Rock Classics

Rolling Stones
Let It Bleed

John Van der Kiste

T0167713

sonicbondpublishing.com

Sonicbond Publishing Limited
www.sonicbondpublishing.co.uk
Email: info@sonicbondpublishing.co.uk

First Published in the United Kingdom 2024
First Published in the United States 2024

British Library Cataloguing in Publication Data:
A Catalogue record for this book is available from the British Library

Copyright John Van der Kiste 2024

ISBN 978-1-78952-309-6

Typeset in ITC Garamond Std & ITC Avant Garde Gothic
Printed and bound in England

Graphic design and typesetting: Full Moon Media

Follow us on social media:
Twitter: https://twitter.com/SonicbondP
Instagram: www.instagram.com/sonicbondpublishing_/
Facebook: www.facebook.com/SonicbondPublishing/

Linktree QR code:

Rolling Stones
Let It Bleed

John Van der Kiste

sonicbondpublishing.com

Rolling Stones
Let It Bleed

Contents

Foreword And Acknowledgements

Even as a 15-year-old leading a somewhat sheltered life with parents and then at boarding school run by masters who regarded The Rolling Stones as a severe threat to western civilisation (much as my contemporaries loved them), during the closing weeks of 1969, it was impossible for us not to be aware of the media hype on radio, TV and in the press that was alerting us to the approaching end of the swinging sixties. The vibrant decade in which it seemed so much had changed beyond recognition was coming to an end. So, it seemed, were The Beatles, whose every new single and album at regular intervals was a major news story in its own right. Was there life in pop music for our generation after The Fab Four?

Yes, there would be. There were still those dreadful, scruffy, libidinous, establishment-baiting, drug-taking Rolling Stones. They were the group you weren't meant to like – but couldn't help liking. There was a kind of almost other-worldly, daredevil excitement, even danger, to most of their records that their Liverpudlian rivals, who always admitted unashamedly that they sang about love, couldn't really match. The Stones also personified a sense of musical adventure, as if to tell us that the Liverpudlian foursome may have been the trailblazers of British pop (the original Britpop group, anyone?), but the London and south-eastern quintet were catching them up fast. Everyone liked most of the songs on *Abbey Road*, but when *Let It Bleed* came into the shops less than three weeks later, there was a rawness, a kind of indefinable mirror-of-the-times to the music that somehow the earlier album couldn't quite equal. A few months later, The Beatles owned up that 'the dream was over'. The Rolling Stones had stayed the course and were now indisputably the world's premier rock 'n' roll band.

More than fifty years later, critics still argue which of their classic four run of albums from 1968 to 1972 was the best. It's a close-run thing, but many still choose *Let It Bleed*, an unchallenged diamond that still goes for the jugular. For many, a teenager of the 1960s turned rock devotee of more senior years, the sheer excitement it captured has never faded.

However, one or two things united my parents, my schoolmasters and myself. None of us ever dreamed that over half a century later I would be writing a book about it, let alone finishing it off in the week that Sir Michael Jagger was celebrating his eightieth birthday – while The Rolling Stones are still a going concern in the music industry, with the release of another album of original material about to be confirmed.

My thanks as ever to Stephen Lambe for commissioning the book, all the editorial staff at Sonicbond, and to my wife Kim for her support as ever during the writing stage.

Introduction

Of The Rolling Stones' 23 studio albums released in Britain, *Let It Bleed* was the eighth. As their American label London had a free hand with their catalogue across the Atlantic, it was their tenth over there. In retrospect, according to general critical opinion, it's the second of four consecutive releases, their best-ever, beginning with *Beggars Banquet* in 1968 and ending with *Exile On Main Street* four years later.

The Rolling Stones were formed in 1962, with Mick Jagger (lead vocals, harmonica), Keith Richards (guitar), Brian Jones (guitar, harmonica), Dick Taylor (bass), later of The Pretty Things, Ian Stewart (piano), and probably Tony Chapman (drums), making their debut on 12 July at the Marquee Club in central London. Drummer Mick Avory had rehearsed with them earlier that year, although he left to join The Kinks shortly before the Stones began playing live. Bill Wyman replaced Taylor in December, and Charlie Watts took over on drums early in 1963. Ian Stewart, their piano player and roadie, the 'sixth Stone' was deemed by their manager Andrew Loog Oldham to be surplus to the band in that five members were enough, and with his heavy build and lantern-jawed face, he was not considered photogenic enough. He accepted this verdict gracefully, and though he never appeared on their album sleeves or in publicity photos, he would remain an ever-dependable, invaluable member of the entourage, as well as playing on stage with them and on nearly every album, until his sudden death after a heart attack in 1985.

Two singles, their version of Chuck Berry's 'Come On' and The Beatles' 'I Wanna be Your Man', followed that year, making number 21 and number 12, respectively, in the charts. Their debut eponymously-named LP, renamed *England's Newest Hitmakers* in the US, with one minor track alteration, appeared in 1964. This consisted of ten cover versions of blues, rock 'n' roll and Motown numbers plus one Jagger-Richards composition and one credited to Nanker Phelge, an alias initially given to compositions from either of the two main writers, or any combination of the group, Stewart included. It topped the British album charts for twelve weeks. Not long afterwards, all group compositions would appear with a Jagger-Richards credit, the vocalist usually being responsible for lyrics and the guitarist the music, although a few were mostly, if not entirely, the work of only one of them. Wyman would later assert that he had come up with the riff on which certain numbers were based, among them 'Paint it Black' and 'Jumpin' Jack Flash', both number one singles that would have earned him substantial royalties as a co-writer had they been attributed more fairly.

As Jagger and Richards's confidence in their songwriting grew, so did the proportion of original material on their records. *Rolling Stones Number Two* and *Out Of Our Heads* both comprised predominantly songs penned by others, although from their 1965 number one 'The Last Time', adapted partly from a traditional gospel song recorded in 1954 by The Staple Singers, until the early 1980s, all A-sides of their singles were Jagger and Richards compositions. So was every track on *Aftermath*, the fourth long player. Regarded as their first 'classic album', it demonstrated their ability to venture beyond the blues and R'n'B influences with its forays into pop, folk, baroque and eastern-influenced music. These were enhanced by Jones's ever-widening use of stringed instruments, as well as koto and marimbas. One track, 'Goin' Home', broke all the rules by being over 11 minutes long, much of it a studio jam on which they just let the tapes roll. Stewart and American session musician and arranger Jack Nitzsche added piano, organ and harpsichord to some numbers. Lyrically, the subject matter of the songs encompassed love and lust, sometimes with a pointedly misogynistic twist and even social comment, as on the most talked-about, 'Mother's Little Helper'. It referred to the prescription pills handed out freely to middle-class housewives, bored with their everyday existence and probably the same people who were hypocritically criticising the younger generation for recreational drug use. Moreover, they were now starting to rival The Beatles in providing hits for more pop-oriented acts. Chris Farlowe, David Garrick, Tony Merrick, and The Searchers all had varying Top 50 success with songs from the album, Farlowe's 'Out of Time' being produced by Jagger and reaching number one, while Wayne Gibson's 'Under My Thumb' became a Northern soul favourite and made number 17 on reissue eight years later.

It was a hard album to follow. *Between The Buttons*, released in January 1967, featured the same line-up plus Stewart and

Nitzsche again, but despite more baroque-tinged pop, folk and even a hint of vaudeville, the songs weren't in the same league. Jagger dismissed it as 'more or less rubbish'. It would also be the final Stones LP with different track listings on the Decca label in Britain and London in America. At the same time, they issued another single, 'Let's Spend the Night Together', an unusually risqué title for the time. In America, the B-side, the less controversially-named, exquisite baroque-sounding ballad 'Ruby Tuesday' was given preference by radio and the *Billboard* charts. The latter song was still credited to Jagger and Richards, although the former admitted he had no hand in writing it, and that it was partly Jones's work.

1967 would be a traumatic year for most of the band. Wyman and Watts, both married and slightly older than the others, kept their distance from the drugs and rock 'n' roll lifestyle, but the remaining three were less circumspect. Drug busts and ensuing court cases dominated newspaper headlines in Britain on an all-too-regular basis. In June, Jagger and Richard were both given jail sentences for breaking the rules, quickly quashed on appeal after the overwhelming view at large suggested that a vindictive establishment was making an example of them. Jones was also arrested, charged with possession and fined but spared imprisonment.

Despite such distractions, they still completed a second new single and album for release later that year. The 45 was promoted as a double A-side, 'Dandelion' embracing the psychedelic whimsy of the time, while 'We Love You' was intended as a thank-you to those who had stood by them during their difficult times. The album, *Their Satanic Majesties Request*, was one that has long divided fans and critics. Some still consider it a major misstep, a half-hearted flower power attempt to jump on the bandwagon or a poor man's *Sergeant Pepper's Lonely Hearts Club Band*, following in the wake of the recent groundbreaking Beatles' album. Others, including this author, regard it as a bold and, for the most part, very enjoyable experiment with different genres, striking songs and arrangements that might have sounded a world away from their early material, a logical development from the direction they had pursued on the previous two albums. It should also be remembered that not only The Beatles but also The Kinks and

The Small Faces were releasing more sophisticated, less rock 'n' roll-orientated product in 1967 somewhat at variance with their singles of two or three years before. Jones was gradually losing interest in playing the guitar and was honing his skill on other instruments, notably mellotron, jew's harp, flute and recorder. One of their engineers said that he could get a musical sound out of anything – even a keyring.

However, at around this time Andrew Loog Oldham, who had produced the previous albums as well as managed them, lost patience with their lack of focus as well as the constant crowd of girlfriends and hangers-on in the studio. Disenchanted with his diminishing support, particularly in their brushes with the law, they terminated their mutual connections, and the result was a record co-produced by the vocalist and the guitarist.

Having decided that *Satanic Majesties* verged on an artistic embarrassment, in 1968, they reverted to form, with their first (brief) live performance for over a year at the *NME* Poll Winners' Concert in May and a return to their blues-rock roots in the studio. That summer, the demonic yet still radio-friendly 'Jumpin' Jack Flash' gave them their first chart-topping single at home for two years. The album *Beggars Banquet*, which their longstanding engineer and, in effect, co-producer Glyn Johns, called it their 'coming of age', and far superior to any of their previous albums, followed that autumn. It would have done sooner but for delays because of their insistence on the notorious 'toilet' sleeve design, on which they were overruled by a cautious Decca. (Some years later, the original cover was allowed on the CD reissue). At around the same time they staged and filmed an extravaganza intended for television, *The Rolling Stones' Rock And Roll Circus*, in which they topped a bill including The Who, Jethro Tull (with temporary guitarist Tony Iommi, shortly to join Black Sabbath), Taj Mahal, and a one-off scratch band, The Dirty Macs, consisting of John Lennon, Eric Clapton, Richards on bass and The Jimi Hendrix Experience's drummer Mitch Mitchell. One year earlier, The Beatles had led the way with *Magical Mystery Tour*. Anywhere the Fab Four led, their rivals would follow.

Jones made his last public performance with the band in this show, and very reluctantly. By now, he was finding himself increasingly marginalised. Having founded the group in the first place, his egocentric attitude towards the others and abusive treatment of successive girlfriends won him no friends, in particular his brief romance with Anita Pallenberg that ended when he beat her up, Richards rescued her and to Jones's fury then formed a relationship with her himself. Once the Jagger-Richards musical partnership had solidified, the band became increasingly their project and no longer his. Wyman, Watts and Stewart were content to go with the flow, but the two frontmen came to resent Jones, once the power base and creative hub had shifted unalterably in their direction. His increasing alcohol and drug abuse and paranoia made him a peripheral, almost superfluous member, little more than a guest musician with what was once his group, a ghostly presence frequently the worse for wear. According to their publicist Keith Altham, by then, he also 'pretty much had the concentration of a mayfly'.

One project to which he devoted serious attention was a field recording of the music of a Moroccan tribe that he had made in July 1968, excerpts from which he initially thought could be integrated into their next album. The idea proved unworkable, though thanks to one of the group's engineers, Alan ('Irish') O'Duffy, about 40 minutes' worth of material was completed and released in 1971 as *Brian Jones Presents The Pipes Of Pan At Joujouka*, on the group's own label (and on the classical outlet Point Records, on CD in 1995), with Jones credited as producer. Although not expected to be a commercial success, it was hailed in retrospect as perhaps the first world music album ever given a major global release. Twenty years later, the Stones revisited the idea and recorded 'Continental Drift', a track on the 1989 album *Steel Wheels*, featuring the musicians from Joujouka.

Jones contributed to eight of the ten tracks on Beggars Banquet, but was increasingly distancing himself and took little part in the recording sessions that he attended all too rarely. 'What can I do, Mick?' he would ask the vocalist. 'Yeah, what can you do, Brian?' was the sneering answer. Sometimes, he would just lie around the studio, reading a magazine. With his increasing lack of self-esteem, erratic mental health and, above all, drug convictions, he was a misfit, if not a liability, and a threat to their plans for another American tour as he would not be granted a work permit. Jimmy Miller, their producer (and occasional percussionist), later pointed out that the important thing about *Let It Bleed* was Richards's amount of work. He took over the group's musical leadership 'and did it brilliantly'. Sometimes he would wonder what Keith could possibly do to make a particular track better, and feared he would overdo it. 'Then suddenly, he'd just play something that would knock me out. It would always be some guitar figure I'd never imagined, which made the whole thing work. That was the magic of the Stones'. Jones was, therefore, redundant.

The band had entered 1969 with what looked like a punishing programme, some details of which were published in the music press. They suggested that a new single would be completed by early May, followed by a second compilation album later that month and a brand new album in June, and the soundtrack to *Rock And Roll Circus* probably in the summer, once it was ready for television. There would be another new single in September, another brand new album by November, and a third new single around the same time. Thanks largely to a chaotic year, only one new single, the compilation album and *Let It Bleed*, one of the new albums, would materialise. *Circus* was shelved indefinitely, after the band saw the results, realised their performance was well below standard, and that they had been completely upstaged by a far superior show from The Who, just off a very successful tour and in far better shape. For years, it was rumoured to have been lost (perhaps conveniently), and finally released in October 1996.

On 8 June 1969, Jagger, Richards and Watts paid a joint visit to Jones at Cotchford Farm, his home in the Sussex countryside, to tell him that he was no longer in the band. His replacement was Mick Taylor, a guitarist who had previously worked with John Mayall, one of the founding fathers of the British blues scene. When he was first contacted by the Stones and came to Olympic Studios, Taylor thought he was just being invited for session work, as Ry Cooder had been, and it was only when they recognised he would be a perfect fit that he realised he was being asked to join as a permanent member. The group informed Jones they would award him a severance payment of £100,000, and a further annual sum of £20,000 for every year that the band continued as a going concern. (Nobody could have envisaged that they would still be performing and recording over fifty years later). How and why he intended to tell the public that he had quit was up to him. Apparently unsurprised and relieved that a difficult decision had been taken out of his hands, he issued a press statement saying he was leaving as he no longer saw eye to eye with the rest of the band on the records they were now making.

One month later, he was found unconscious in his swimming pool, and pronounced dead on arrival at hospital. The official verdict was 'death by misadventure', despite a persistent theory that he had been murdered by a builder who was working on his house and had allegedly been fired yet was still owed a considerable sum of money. Coincidentally the day that he died, 3 July, was one day before the release of their new single, 'Honky Tonk Women'. They had begun recording it in March and he was present at the early sessions, although he did not contribute anything. Most of the guitar work on the record had been that of Richards, with overdubs added by Taylor shortly after he joined.

To introduce their new member to the public, the band had scheduled a free concert in Hyde Park, London, on 5 July. They were to top a bill with several other acts, including Family, King Crimson and Third Ear Band. At first, they considered cancelling it altogether as a mark of respect, especially as the funeral was not to take place until five days afterwards. But they decided to play regardless, explaining that it was to be a tribute to Jones – or else, as the cynical may have said, as a demonstration that it was 'business as usual'. A film of the performance, first shown on television two months later, and subsequently released on home video, revealed a comparatively lacklustre performance. Jagger was suffering from hay fever and laryngitis, and five numbers were considered so bad that they were omitted altogether. Ian Stewart said it was the worst show they'd ever given, although his explanation that they hadn't even rehearsed wasn't strictly accurate. Nevertheless, on what was meant to be their first full-length gig for over two years, they were clearly not on form. The 14-song set included 'Honky Tonk Women', plus just two of the songs that would appear on *Let It Bleed*, 'Love in Vain' and 'Midnight Rambler'.

Sessions for the album had begun late the previous year with the initial working title *Automatic Changer*, although Richards wanted *Hard Knox And Durty Sox*, which would survive as a subtitle long enough to appear on the inner bag credits. Jones had played autoharp on one track, and contributed percussion to another. Mick Taylor added overdubs on two tracks, but most guitar work and some of the bass was by Keith Richards. A change in title was agreed, and in the process it became the first Rolling Stones album to take its name from one of the tracks.

John Lennon once said that when The Beatles sneezed, The Rolling Stones caught a cold – sitar on 'Norwegian Wood', followed by 'Paint it Black'; 'All You Need is Love', then 'We Love You'; *Sergeant Pepper*, then *Their Satanic Majesties Request*; plain white sleeves with minimal lettering on the front for *The Beatles* ('White Album'), then *Beggars Banquet*. This time, the Stones stole a march on their rivals. The Liverpool quartet had recorded 'Let it Be' at the beginning of the year and acetates were circulated around the music industry soon afterwards. As both bands were managed at the time by Allen Klein, news of forthcoming projects was shared between them and each had advance notice of what the other camp was doing. But the 'Let it Be' single and its parent album were not released until the spring of 1970, a few months after *Let It Bleed*. When Richards was interviewed by Robert Greenfield of *Rolling Stone* in 1971, he hinted that it might have been coincidence – or maybe not. They didn't know what to call the completed but still unnamed track, he said, and it almost became 'When You Need Someone', or 'Take my Arm, Take my Leg'. 'Maybe there was some influence,' he conceded, 'because *Let It Be* had been kicked around for years for their movie, for that album'. To say 'years' suggests exaggeration, but the idea may have been there, maybe even as a joke.

Let It Bleed, and *Through The Past, Darkly,* the second compilation of hits and choice album tracks that had reached the shops three months earlier, were the last studio albums released by Decca with The Rolling Stones' full approval. The live set, *Get Yer Ya-Ya's Out!*, followed on the same label in 1970. All their official releases for the next few years would be on their own imprint, Rolling Stones Records, while Decca continued to put out several exploitative, poorly-designed sets with ill-considered track listings that annoyed them intensely as they were never consulted first.

Let It Bleed was one of the last major releases from their original company to appear in mono (red label) as well as stereo (blue label), at a time when the other leading companies had moved over completely to stereo. Mono pressings were only on sale for a short period, and highly collectable a few years hence. All copies came in a single outer sleeve plus a flimsy inner red or blue bag, with one side containing the then standard information about record playing equipment, record care and mono/stereo, and the other side full track-by-track credits, not always accurately. Some names were given or spelt wrongly, notably those of Mary [sic] Clayton, Madelaine [sic] Bell, and Nanette Workman, the American backing vocalist who appeared on two tracks, and who had been confused with British actress Nanette Newman, an error seemingly not corrected on later pressings or issues, either on LP or CD. (One of the engineers said that whoever provided the credits must have been stoned at the time). After a couple of years, the vinyl inner bag came with one side blank and, therefore, no credits. The name of The London Bach Choir was visible only on the earliest printings of the inner and later blacked out (as it was on my copy, purchased brand new over the counter about six weeks after release), allegedly because they didn't want their name associated with the band whose name was still not always a suitable subject for conversation in polite company, and because they found the lyrical content of three tracks objectionable.

Jagger had originally asked the Swiss artist M. C. Escher, whose illustration of lizards crawling across a book had adorned the front of the debut album by Mott The Hoople earlier that year, to design the sleeve, but he declined. Richards then asked graphic designer Robert Brownjohn to suggest an idea, and though the title was altered from their original choice of *Automatic Changer*, they were so impressed with his work that they retained it. He deliberately altered the track order on the back, as for aesthetic reasons, he preferred the titles spaced that way. The cake, with five tiny toy model figures representing each of the group on the icing, perched on top of a car tyre, a pizza, a clockface, a film canister all on a plate, with a record and a very old arm with enormous 78 r.p.m. record needle underneath, had been baked by the then up-and-coming Delia Smith. At the time, she was working, she said, as 'a jobbing home economist' with a food photographer who shot for commercials and magazines, prior to becoming a renowned cookbook writer and TV celebrity. Everything is in order on the front, but turn it over and a slice has been cut out, four of the figures have fallen over (leaving only the one representing Richards still standing), and all supporting items are smashed.

A colour poster of the group, folded in four, was included and mentioned on a removable sticker on the sleeve. The design showed a large head and shoulders image of Jagger, facing to the left, as the background to a picture of all five seated on the ground. It was based on one taken at a photo shoot at Hyde Park on 13 June 1969, the day they announced Mick Taylor as their newest member.

Let It Bleed

Tracklisting:

Gimme Shelter ['Gimmie Shelter' on early and some subsequent pressings] 4.30

Love In Vain (Woody Payne) 4.18

Country Honk 3.00

Live With Me 3.35

Let It Bleed 5.27

Midnight Rambler 6.52

You Got The Silver 2.51

Monkey Man 4.12

You Can't Always Get What You Want 7.28

All written by Mick Jagger and Keith Richards except 'Love In Vain'. 'Woody Payne' was a pseudonym for Robert Johnson, whose name appeared on some later pressings.

Album Credits

Personnel:

Group:

Mick Jagger: lead vocal (all but 7), harp (harmonica) (1, 6)

Keith Richards: lead vocal (7), backing vocal (1, 3, 4, 8), electric guitar (all but 3), slide guitar (2, 5, 6, 7,8), acoustic guitar (2, 3, 5, 7, 9), bass (4)

Mick Taylor: slide guitar (3), electric guitar (4)

Brian Jones: congas (6), autoharp (7)

Bill Wyman: bass (all but 3, 4), vibraphone (8)

Charlie Watts: drums (all but 9)

Additional artists:

Ian Stewart: piano (5)

Nicky Hopkins: piano (1, 4, 7, 8), organ (7)

Ry Cooder: mandolin (2)

Bobby Keys: tenor saxophone (4)

Jimmy Miller: percussion – guiro, maracas (1), tambourine (8), drums (9)

Al Kooper: piano, organ, French horn (9)

Leon Russell: piano, horn arrangement (4)

Merry Clayton: vocals (1)

Nanette Workman: backing vocals (3, 9) – wrongly credited as
Nanette Newman
Doris Troy, Madeline Bell: backing vocals (9)
Rocky Dijon: percussion (9)
Jack Nitzsche: choral arrangements (9)
London Bach Choir (9)

Producer: Jimmy Miller
Chief Engineer: Glyn Johns
Assistant engineers: Bruce Botnick, Jerry Hansen, George Chkiantz,
Alan ('Irish') O'Duffy

Recorded at Olympic Studios, London; Elektra Sound Recorders,
and (perhaps, disputed) Sunset Sound, both Los Angeles,
November 1968-November 1969
Record labels (original): Decca (UK), London (US); later ABKCO,
now Universal
Release dates: 28 November 1969 (US), 5 December 1969 (UK)
Highest chart positions: 1 (UK), 2 (US)
Running time: 42:13 (20:50 side 1, 21:23 side 2)

The Recording Of The Album

Sessions for the album, or at least one track, probably began in the late autumn of 1968, just as the release of *Beggars Banquet* was imminent. There are conflicting theories about 'You Got The Silver', taped at Olympic Studios, Barnes, London, under the original title of 'You Got Some Silver Now'. Some sources say it was recorded or at least started around May and June that year, others that it was not begun until February 1969 or perhaps slightly earlier. What is certain is that by now the group had got in the habit of recording more tracks for an album that they needed at any one set of sessions, especially as the limitations of the long-playing record allowed for only twenty minutes or so of music per side before sound quality and volume began to deteriorate. The 26 minutes on each side of *Aftermath* in 1966, the UK release, was an interesting (and rare if not unique) outlier. Songs would often be shelved and appear on an album some years later, often but not always reworked to some extent and sometimes completely renamed in the process. A few tracks on *Sticky Fingers* and *Exile On Main St* had been started much earlier, and either took a little longer to see the light of day or else underwent a certain amount of fine-tuning and development before they were considered ready for release.

None of the recent remastered reissues of *Let It Bleed* have included any early demos or alternate versions, outtakes and the like. While The Beatles supplemented a 50th anniversary reissue of their 'White Album' in 2018 with an additional 27-track CD of 'Esher Demos' and further discs containing previously unavailable material, as well as having put out other long-archived items on the three *Anthology* releases in 1995 and 1996, there was little if anything left in the Rolling Stones' vaults from the 1968-69 period, after the appearance in 1975 of *Metamorphosis*, a 16-track collection of odds and ends taped between 1964 and 1969. Another reason is that both bands went about recording albums of original material in a very different way. Most new Beatles songs had been wholly or partly written by John Lennon, Paul McCartney or George Harrison, and their creator would bring them to the studio so that the other three, and producer-cum-arranger George Martin, could help guide and shape each one through several recorded versions, up to 20 or more, transforming the basic lyrics and melody into a fully-fledged single or album cut. The Stones had a more free and easy approach in that they would start jamming in the studio, throwing in ideas, riffs and so on, as a basic song gradually developed. Most of them would make some contribution, although the end result was nearly always credited to Jagger and Richards, sometimes much to the frustration of Wyman or Taylor, whose input, had they belonged to any other band, would almost certainly have resulted in their name appearing on the record label in brackets afterwards and thus composers' royalties. Richards would claim that he used to set up the riffs, the hook and sometimes the title, and it was Mick's job as a wordsmith to fill in the rest. As a result, few out-takes or discards were left over, and almost everything not used for the next album was kept to be reworked, recycled or taken to pieces and started again.

When asked in 1995, in the wake of The Beatles' Anthology, why there was no unreleased Stones material being put out, their former manager Allen Klein said there wasn't any. He only wanted their fans to hear what was worth hearing. If it wasn't made available at the time, then it probably wasn't worth doing so at all. How many early versions or remixes did the most devoted listener really want? 'Collectors want every scrap to come out. I don't'. In the case of *Let It Bleed*, there had been one unique exception, a tape of jams made one day that Richards unusually absented himself, that would be selected for standalone release a couple of years later as *Jamming With Edward!*

Sessions for the album began in earnest on 16 November, three weeks before the release of *Beggars Banquet*, with the basic track of 'You Can't Always Get What You Want'. It was recorded with Richards on acoustic guitar, Al Kooper on piano, Wyman on bass, and Miller on drums, with Jagger singing what everyone assumed was just a guide vocal. Kooper's contribution to the song would be pivotal, and his presence in the right place at the right time was the result of a happy accident. He was already a legendary figure in America after having contributed organ to Bob Dylan's 'Like a Rolling Stone', playing with Dylan's band at the historic Newport Folk Festival in 1965, at which the songwriter was almost booed off stage, and then for production work with his own two bands, Blues Project and Blood, Sweat and Tears, and also with The Zombies on *Odessey And Oracle*. Exhausted and in need of a vacation, he took himself to London for a spell, during which he had decided he would have nothing to do with music. On arriving in England, he was picked up by his friend, fellow producer Denny Cordell, who told him that The Rolling Stones had heard he was coming and wanted to book him for two days' worth of studio work. He firmly refused, but while walking down Kings Road, he bumped into Brian Jones, who told him they were all expecting him and really excited at the prospect of being able to work together. With that, he decided he could hardly let them down.

Kooper listened to a run-through of the song, which he thought sounded quite folky at first, and immediately put forward a few suggestions. He said it would be better with more of an R'n'B style, similar to that of Etta James's version of the Sonny and Cher hit 'I Got You Babe', and some samba percussion. Also at the studio that day were Doris Troy and Madeline Bell, both of whom were among the most in-demand session backing vocalists of the time, and Nanette Workman, a friend of assistant engineer Vic Smith, all available to contribute. Ironically, according to Kooper, as Jagger and Richards were really producing everything themselves, Miller wasn't really adding anything to justify the credit he was being given. He did, however, play the drums on this song. Frustrated in getting the feel he wanted for the track, he approached Watts, who was having some difficulty in playing exactly what Miller had suggested. In retrospect, it seems strange that a producer should be trying to tell one of Britain's most respected rock and jazz musicians how to do his own job, but early in the session, Miller asked if he could sit at the drums for a minute to show him exactly what he had in mind. Watts agreed to let him, stood and watched, and said quite placidly, 'Well, why don't you just play it?' Kooper was amazed, saying afterwards that he thought Miller was determined to be credited on the recording somehow as musician as well as producer, and it would, therefore, have made no difference how well Watts had played.

After the basic track was done, they began overdubbing, with Richards adding more electric guitar, and Kooper organ to supplement what he had already put down on piano. These additions, the latter said, 'brought it up a few notches', and afterwards, he told Jagger to let him know if he wanted horns on it. However, at the time, everyone assumed that the track was more or less done, apart from the lead vocal. Subsequent work would transform it into one of the most epic recordings of the decade, but at this stage, it was put on one side for further development. Kooper also suggested adding French horn, which he did himself and scored arrangements for further horns, trumpets and saxophone. He added them to the backing track after returning to Los Angeles, and was puzzled when he heard the completed album and found they had only kept the French horn.

A break for other activities, including rehearsals for and filming of *The Rolling Stones Rock And Roll Circus* at Intertel Studios, Wembley, in December, put sessions on hold for several weeks. 'You Can't Always Get What You Want' was about to receive its public premiere at the start of their seven-song set, a spirited performance but as yet giving little idea of its potential, of what the finished recording would sound like. They were all fired up when they returned to Olympic on 10 February 1969 for weeks of solid work that included several of the basic tracks for the rest of the album (and some for the next two after that), as well as for the 'Honky Tonk Women' single.

'You Got the Silver' had been started the previous year, and was first on the list for working on further. A gentle, relaxed love song, it was written entirely by Richards, and the subject was Anita Pallenberg. Marianne Faithfull confirmed as much; 'the depth of his attachment to her was just flowing out of him'. In his memoir *Life*, some thirty years later, he confirmed that it was all his own work, and sang it solo 'simply because we had to spread the workload'. Almost from the start, he and Jagger had been singing harmonies, like the Everly Brothers, so for him to take the lead vocal should hardly have been a surprise to anyone. It also featured autoharp played by Jones, one of the last contributions he ever made to the band. It had been agreed by Jagger and Richards that if Jones really wanted to try and play anything on a track, no matter how strange or experimental it might seem at the time, they would let him. It was as if they wanted to give him a chance to prove that he was still capable of some contribution on his 'more together' days, with the understanding that they could always wipe it again afterwards if it was unsuitable. On the rare occasions when he turned up at the studio and picked up his guitar, an instrument in which he seemed to have lost interest, Richards would ensure that his amp was turned off and he never seemed to notice.

Later that week, they began work on 'Give Me Some Shelter', which later become 'Gimme Shelter' or even 'Gimmie Shelter' on early pressings. This was another song apparently written completely by Richards on his own, and an early version features his lead vocal. Part of the sound was obtained through his experiments with some Triumph amps. Probably by a happy accident, he and the engineer George Chkiantz between them found that they had lights along the top, and that the amps themselves would produce 'an amazing crunch' once they got to a certain stage of overheating, would then turn themselves off or blow up, and they could tell because that was then the lights dimmed. They had to be at exactly the right volume, and going like that for the right amount of time, and the sound they made was quite extraordinary. All they needed to do to get it was 'bash the amps around a bit'. They also had to be ready at the precise moment, once they had reached the right temperature, then allowed to cool down for a bit and were reheated.

Another key to the instrumental sounds on the recording of this song was Jagger's harmonica, put through limiters and other devices which required distortion caused by overdriving an old Dynacord tape loop machine. Yet another vital ingredient was the piano work of another keyboard player, Nicky Hopkins. He was already a legend in the music business after working with others, including The Beatles, The Who, The Kinks and The Move. A gentle character, less abrasive than Ian Stewart, who would make his feelings known when he disliked anything the band wanted to play (notably songs that had minor chords), his style fitted in perfectly to the extent that he, too, became almost another 'sixth Stone'. The band spent some time on this number, and a couple of other early versions have emerged, illustrating a work in progress but somehow lacking the feeling of menace they eventually captured, all featuring just male vocals. One of the crucial ingredients would come when the song was revisited a few months later. Finally, on the recording, Richards used an Australian hollow-body guitar, a Maton SE777, that was about to give up the ghost. He later related to Guitar World that on the final note of the song, the neck of the instrument fell off, and the noise could be heard on early takes of the song.

The band always worked hard to achieve exactly the right effect, for other songs that were started in the February and March period, and before, would be left and completed after a gap of several months. In March, they also began 'Honky Tonk Women', which would become a standalone single, the basic track of 'Midnight Rambler', and supposedly a mainly instrumental number initially called 'If You Need Someone' and would become 'Let It Bleed'.

'You Can't Always Get What You Want' was another that they returned to after an interval of some weeks. Had the band been content to issue a studio recording of the song that had received its debut on the *Rock And Roll Circus,* it would have been understandable, but they realised the version they had begun work on the previous year still had potential for much more. They discussed putting strings on it, but then somebody, probably Jagger, had the idea of adding a complete choir, probably the first for a rock band. It was initially deemed too ambitious, until Nitzsche suggested it would be simple enough to get the London Bach Choir. Fifty of the singers were booked to turn up – and sixty arrived. Much to engineer George Chkiantz's amusement, they turned up with a crate of milk bottles, as if on a primary school outing. Nitzsche had worked out a choral arrangement, and they took their places at Olympic, the band of musicians in clouds of smoke in the control room, with the choristers at the other end of the studio, each unit separated by fifty feet of no-man's land.

But in this case, the Stones, one might say, would take a long song, and make it better. Once the tape was rolling, Jagger said he wished he could get them to sing it a cappella without the backing track. Although unsure how to ask them, he need not have worried. Having seemingly got bored by the waiting around and doing nothing, and once they had done their work on the finale, to keep themselves amused, they started an unaccompanied version of the opening verse. That was also recorded and would be added at the start of the song, prior to the subdued intro on acoustic guitar and first verse, with the sixty voices double-tracked to make it sound like there were even more of them. Jagger also tried to get them to vary their accent slightly by singing the words with more of a drawl, but with little success.

Yet, as Kooper observed of the extra choral material, 'It made no sense whatsoever, but it was terrific'. He subsequently added piano, organ and French horn, while Doris Troy, Madeline Bell and Nanette Workman also joined in to swell the choruses. Further work took place on 'You Got The Silver', perhaps an alternate take, with Jagger on vocal, Nicky Hopkins on piano and organ.

Sessions spread out over the next month included 'Sister Morphine', a song supposed to have been co-written by Jagger, Richards and Marianne Faithfull, who was the singer's girlfriend at the time. Another version of the story is that they added Faithfull's name to the credits in order to bring a few composer's royalties her way, and yet another has it that she genuinely co-wrote the song but was removed from the credits because they wanted to avoid any monies being paid to an agent with whom she was in dispute at the time. It was released as a B-side to her version of a Gerry Goffin-Barry Mann song, 'Something Better', with both sides produced by Jagger, and hastily withdrawn by Decca a couple of days later when they looked at the title of the B-side. The band later recorded 'Sister Morphine' themselves for the next album, *Sticky Fingers*, released in 1971. Also thought to have been recorded at around this time was 'I Was Just a Country Boy', or at least a backing track that may have been shelved altogether or later reworked under another title entirely. The main product of this period, however, was the only non-original track, 'Love in Vain'. Originally 'Love in Vain Blues', it was written and recorded in 1937 by Robert Johnson, the 'king of the blues singers', shortly before his early death, but credited to Woody Payne, a pseudonym used by a music publisher of Johnson's songs.

American session guitarist and later a much-acclaimed solo performer in his own right, Ry Cooder, played mandolin on the song, one of the first times the instrument had featured so prominently on a rock record. But his experiences as a Rolling Stone guest would always leave him with a bitter aftertaste. Later that year, he declared that the band's management had brought him to England under false pretences, asked him to play on the session because they weren't doing so particularly well themselves, and were just messing around in the studio. When there was a lull in rehearsals, he would play his guitar and Richards would go away. It later transpired that they had left the tapes running in order to record everything he played. He alleged that Richards simply listened to and merely copied what he was playing, and based the riff they used on 'Honky Tonk Women' on one of his progressions. Richards was startled by his words, but admitted that Cooder's style did influence him in his decision to use the open G tuning on 'Gimme Shelter' and other songs, as well as a five-string guitar regularly afterwards.

Another song done at this time was a Wyman composition, a Mockney knees-up novelty that brought the Small Faces to mind, with lead vocal by Jagger. Initially called 'Lyle Street Lucie', it was rejected as substandard and would end up as 'Downtown Suzie' on *Metamorphosis* six years later. Thereafter, sessions continued on a stop-start basis, resulting in the completion of 'Let It Bleed', and 'Midnight Rambler'. The backing track for the latter had already been started and was worked up into a complete song by Jagger and Richards in April while they were on holiday in Italy.

Numerous tracks were started, and sometimes discarded or perhaps filed away or future development, between May and July. One reason for the delay was the ever-growing problem of Jones's future and, as far as the remaining four were concerned, his replacement. Once Mick Taylor was confirmed as the new Rolling Stone in June, 'Honky Tonk Women' was completed with his help, as well as additional saxophone from Steve Gregory and Bud Beadle, and backing vocals from Madeline Bell and female trio Reparata and The Delrons. An acoustic country-folk version, 'Country Honk', played in the style of Hank Williams and Jimmie Rodgers, and on which he played acoustic slide guitar, was also taped.

Other songs from this period included 'Monkey Man', recorded in two stints, one in late April and the second between June and the beginning of July, and a cover version of Stevie Wonder's 'I Don't Know Why', the song they were working on at Olympic the night that they were phoned at the studio with news of Jones's death. It would appear as a little-noticed single in 1973 after the group were no longer on Decca Records, with minor success in the US but none in the UK, and two years later on *Metamorphosis*.

This latter album would also include 'I'm Going Down', one of only two songs on which Taylor was ever given a joint writer's credit with Jagger and Richards, and on which Stephen Stills was in the studio and may have also played on, and 'Jiving Sister Fanny'. 'Loving Cup' was not only premiered at the Hyde Park show but also held over for *Exile On Main St* in 1972. A few more unreleased (or maybe later reworked and renamed) cuts, such as 'Curtis Meets Smokey', 'Mucking About', 'Toss the Coin', 'Old Vulture', and 'Old Glory', or 'When Old Glory Comes Along', date from this time, most if not all thought to feature Taylor on guitar. Others, possibly dating from a few months earlier, included 'Too Many Cooks'. 'Two Train Blues'. 'Red Blood Wine', 'Stuck Out All Alone', and 'Walking Through the Sleepy City'.

'Honky Tonk Women' was released on 4 July. It gave them an unprecedented five-week run at Number one in Britain during July and August and four weeks in America. After the Hyde Park concert, Jagger went to Australia for the filming of *Ned Kelly*. While he was there, it has been told, Miller and Johns were mixing 'You Got the Silver', and the former thought they should put some reverse echo on the lead guitar. To achieve this, they had to turn the tape upside down and play it backwards while putting echo on the guitar and recording the return from the chamber on an empty track. Johns worked out which was the empty track to record on, and later discovered he had inadvertently erased the vocals. Getting Jagger back to England in a hurry to redo it was impracticable, so they asked Richards, who had, after all, written the song, to step up for what was to date only his second lead vocal on a group album.

This was the version of events as given in Johns's memoirs, but some have expressed their doubts. A good quality bootleg version featuring Jagger's vocals is known to exist. In any case, if this version had been lost, it could have been re-recorded, or his voice overdubbed on the backing track when the band went to America in mid-October. Their purpose was twofold; they were going on tour, and also had to complete recording and mixing the album at Elektra and Sunset Sound Studios. Engineer Bruce Botnick later claimed that all the American work was done only at Elektra. 'Gimme Shelter' was finished with participation from Merry Clayton and 'Country Honk' with Byron Berline, as related below.

At least two other numbers planned for the album were thought to have been recorded in Los Angeles about this time, although sources suggest they may have been done or at least stated earlier in the year. Jagger had begun writing 'Got a Line on You' the previous year as a kind of plea to Jones to get himself together. Under the title '(Can't Seem to) Get a Line on You', it was recorded by the group with Leon Russell on piano during sessions for the latter's eponymously-named solo album issued in 1970. This version didn't find a full release until added as a bonus track on a 1993 reissue. Meanwhile, the band had reworked it as 'Shine a Light' and issued it on *Exile On Main St.* Much the same happened to 'All Down the Line', first recorded in an acoustic version, then considered for *Sticky Fingers* and finally included on *Exile On Main St.*

An 11-minute number, 'Hillside Blues' / 'I Don't Know the Reason Why', is basically a blues jam that has been bootlegged and uploaded online, though never officially issued. While it might have benefited from a little editing, it is worth hearing for the interplay between Richards and Taylor from the point at around six minutes in. The main bootlegs, all named *The Alternate Let It Bleed*, were issued in Europe around 2013, one being a single picture disc album with a cake and LP design loosely based on the original, and the others being double albums on various colours of vinyl. Track listings vary slightly, but they include mostly outtakes from the Olympic sessions from February to October 1969 and a few live recordings from the American tour. The studio cuts include tracks that later appeared, maybe in slightly different forms, on *Exile On Main St.* and *Metamorphosis*, as well as 'I Don't Care', Who Am I (See I Love You)', a blues jam 'I Ain't Lyin'', and a couple of instrumentals, 'Leather Jacket' and 'Dancing in the Light'. These may have been just working titles for unfinished numbers that were later reworked and would appear on later releases under different names.

Jamming With Edward!

Although most of the tracks recorded at around this time would be worked on further and sharpened up for albums in the next few years, there was an intriguing curiosity, almost an elephant in the Stones' room, in the shape of one day's worth of 'unofficial' studio material that would make it on to vinyl and later on CD more or less as it was recorded. On 23 April 1969, Richards failed to turn up for a session at Olympic, thought to be because Glyn Johns had brought Ry Cooder along to help fill out the sound of a band that had been temporarily reduced to one guitarist. Jagger was developing his skills on the instrument as a rhythm player as well as on piano, and would receive a credit for his guitar work on *Sticky Fingers* and several subsequent albums. However, the days when he would play either instrument on stage were still some way ahead, and as a guitarist, he never aspired to be in the same league as his songwriting partner. But as three of the group as well as Cooder and Hopkins, had already arrived, and there was nothing else for them to do, they decided they might as well plug their instruments in and jam together. Johns let the tapes roll, put them away and forgot about them for a while. On returning to them a couple of years later, he was pleasantly surprised to find that he had in front of him a perfectly acceptable, if by no means outstanding, album almost ready to go. He mixed the results and the record went on sale at mid-price in January 1972, as *Jamming With Edward!* (*Waiting For Keith* might have been a better title, but may not have gone down well with the absent guitarist). It didn't really warrant releasing really, he said later, 'but it was okay, a bit of fun, and there's some good playing on it'.

Hopkins was in two minds about it, telling *Disc And Music Echo*:

It was simply a neat thing to do. It's not really a Stones record. We use about half the jam on the record. We thought people might like to hear what goes down between actual recording proper. But it's not a serious album by any means, and I'd hate people to say, 'is this the best Nicky Hopkins can do?'

The title was chosen because it was regarded to some extent as Hopkins's album. One day not long before, Jones (playing bass) and the keyboard player were at opposite ends of the studio, and Jones called out to him, 'Give me an E, Nicky'. He couldn't hear, so Jones then shouted, 'Give me an E for Edward'. The name simply stuck. The result is a fairly loose, relaxed Rolling Stones album without Richards, or if you like, *Let It Bleed*'s baby brother. It obviously can't be judged alongside the other band albums, but long players with tracks including lengthy improvisatory passages were not uncommon in the late 1960s and early 1970s, such as Pink Floyd's *Ummagumma* for example and the 'Apple Jam' third vinyl disc in George Harrison's *All Things Must Pass*.

The lengthy 'Edward's Thrump Up' and 'Blow With Ry' drag a little in paces, but such music is invariably more fun for the musicians playing it than listeners at home, whose attention may start wandering or merely be waiting for a chorus they can join in with. On the other hand, anyone who likes to hear them sing the blues will relish the Elmore James song 'It Hurts Me Too', that suddenly starts quoting from Bob Dylan's 'Pledging My Time'. 'Boudoir Stomp' sounds rather like a dress rehearsal for the much longer 'Midnight Rambler' with its subtle rhythmic changes, although the piano and harmonica are much more prominent, particularly in the first couple of minutes. Moreover, the sudden transition on 'Highland Fling' from a Scottish tune familiar to nearly everyone since childhood to a sprightly 12-bar blues played as a jazz shuffle can't help but bring a smile to the listener's face. Much the same can be said for the two-minute 'Interlude a la El Hopo', part of which is built playfully around the old late 19th century waltz 'The Loveliest Night of the Year', before descending into an anarchic free-for-all.

As Johns admitted with understatement, 'there's some good playing on it' as well as a certain amount of fooling around. It sounded like they were enjoying themselves and yet still coming across like true professional musicians to their fingertips for most of the time. Stones fans and blues lovers, at least, will surely prefer something like this over the portentous, protracted epics that dominate much of *Ummagumma*. Jagger's sleeve note in which he said he hoped that buyers would spend longer listening to it than they did recording it may not have been such a vain one as he might have supposed. Critics were dismissive if not hostile at the time, and in a retrospective feature nearly thirty years later,

Above: Clockwise from top left:
Bill Wyman, Keith Richards and
Mick Taylor.

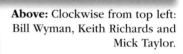

Left: Mick Jagger.

Above and below: Robert Brownjohn's sleeve design for the album, featuring a cake baked by the then-little-known Delia Smith, later renowned cook and TV presenter. (*Decca / London*)

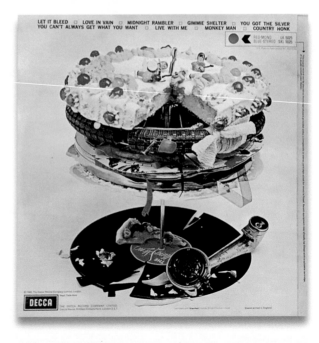

Right: A poster enclosed with initial copies of the album, designed by Victor Kahn, based on the June 1969 press conference photo [see page four of colour insert].

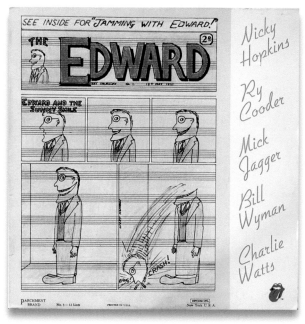

Left: The cover of *Jamming With Edward!* features sleeve drawings by Nicky Hopkins, who was credited with lead billing on the album.

Left: An American music press advert for the album.

Above: The Rolling Stones at a press conference at Hyde Park, at which Mick Taylor was announced as their new guitarist [see previous page].

Right: Richard Green's enthusiastic, if somewhat bland, review of the album in the *New Musical Express*, 29 November 1969.

Below: Keith Richards, producer Jimmy Miller and Mick Jagger at Elektra Studios, Los Angeles.

NEW MUSIC

On sale, Friday, week ending November 29, 1969

GREAT STONES ALBUM!

declares RICHARD GREEN

ROLLING STONES: LET IT BLEED (Decca mono and stereo SKL/LK 5025; 37s 6d. Released December 5).

WHAT a great album! The Stones have obviously put a lot of thought and hard work into it and I have no hesitation in naming it one of the Top Five LPs of 1969—people are going to have to go a long way to beat it.

There's so much variety that each track makes you want to hear it again and again. The late Brian Jones is heard on a couple of numbers and Mick Taylor appears on his first Stones album. It's really an incredible piece of work that shows the group and friends at their best.

GIMME SHELTER. This is one of the Stones' mid-tempo specialities with a heavy beat and tons of oomph. Mick sings the first part and is then joined by Keith and Mary Clayton, before an easy guitar break that leads into a yelling solo by Mary. The whole thing becomes louder and wilder with Mick playing harmonica and the rhythm section letting rip.

LOVE IN VAIN. A slow, heavy ballad with a Hawaiian guitar effect and some nice mandolin work by Ry Cooder. Mick's voice is in its rough and mournful mood as he sings about following his baby to the station only to see her leave on a train. It's all very woeful and very appealing.

COUNTRY HONK. Grab your partners, folk, for the hoe-down version of " Honky Tonk Women." A gas of a track, with Byron Berline on fiddle and Nanette Newman joining Mick and Keith on vocals. Mick Taylor appears on slide guitar and Charlie Watts gets a nice tapping beat going to hold the whole thing together. A fine number

LIVE WITH ME. " Don't you think there's a place for you in between the sheets" sings Mick, so we all know what this one's about. The whole works are thrown in, including horns arranged by Leon Russell, who also plays piano with Nicky Hopkins, Bobby Keys' tenor sax gives a tremendous bite to the unrestrained sound that ends in a massive free for all.

LET IT BLEED. A lot like the first track in style, but with Ian Stewart's piano playing a large part and Bill Wyman on autoharp as well as bass. Keith gets some good sound from his guitar which butts in now and then with a series of phrases and his solo leads. Charlie and Ian into a constrained rave up. Keith begins to dominate the proceedings again towards the end and though it's five minutes, twenty seven seconds long, you want to hear more.

MIDNIGHT RAMBLER. The original Stones, with Brian Jones on percussion. Again, it's Keith who comes through strongest while Mick sings a medium-fast lyric and plays harmonica

About midway, it quietens and there's some nice interplay between guitar and harmonica, then the whole caboodle speeds up and Mick's voice can just be heard beneath the action. A sudden switch to a slow, quiet section which only serves as an intro to more raverama. Much long and much good.

YOU GOT THE SILVER. Short and Dylan-ish, with Keith singing and even sounding a bit like Dylan. There are odd bits of what sounds like an acoustic twelve-string guitar breaking up the song which is a change from the Stones' usual style but which shows their versatility.

MONKEE MAN. Medium tempo with lots of instrumental work which gives Keith plenty of room to work out and Charlie

gets his oar in with some nice playing. Mick begins yelling like an enraged chimp at the end as, again, all hell break loose.

YOU CAN'T ALWAYS GET WHAT YOU WANT. Ye Gods! The London Bach Choir; Madeline Bell, Doris Troy and Nanette Newman! Al Kooper on piano, French horn and organ, and Jimmy Miller on drums. It starts off like a chorale, then Mick takes over as the tempo increases slightly. The girls join him for the title line which is repeated over and over and that works well. There's a part about the Chelsea Drugstore and an "angel chorus" backing heart goings-on in the long track full of surprises and a credit to producer Jimmy Miller and all involved!

ROLLING STONES LET IT BLEED

Symbolistic? The front cover of the STONES' " Let It Bleed " LP shows them as figures on a wedding cake. Then everything goes wrong, as depicted on the back cover, below.

Left: A poster for the Oakland Coliseum Concert, 9 November 1969, where the bootleg *Live'r Than You'll Never Be* was recorded.

Below: The band during a rehearsal at Saville Theatre, London, December 1969.

Above: Mick Taylor, Charlie Watts and Mick Jagger on stage at Hyde Park on 5 July 1969, Taylor's live debut with the band.

Left: Jagger and Richards at Hyde Park.

Above: A completist's dream – the 50th-anniversary deluxe edition, limited to 27,000 hand-numbered copies, 2019.

Record Collector opined unforgivingly that 'even at budget price, it was a rip-off,' but longstanding fans who are discovering it for the first time might be pleasantly surprised. It was reissued some twenty years later on CD after the Stones had signed to Virgin Records, although nobody ever took it to its arguably logical conclusion by including it as a double, an extra disc like The Beatles' *Fly On The Wall* packaged with *Let It Be...Naked,* or even, at a pinch, a 79-minute CD with the nine original tracks on *Let It Bleed.* But Richards would undoubtedly have said no.

Personnel:
Nicky Hopkins: keyboards, piano, sleeve design
Ry Cooder: guitars
Mick Jagger: vocals, harmonica
Bill Wyman: bass guitar
Charlie Watts: drums
Produced by Glyn Johns
Recorded at Olympic Studio, London, April 1969
Record label: Rolling Stones Records (Virgin, 1995 reissue)
Release date: January 1972
Highest chart positions: – (UK); 33 (US)
Running time: 36:05
All tracks written by Ry Cooder, Nicky Hopkins and Charlie Watts unless stated otherwise

Tracklisting:
1. The Boudoir Stomp 5.13
2. It Hurts Me Too (Elmore James / Mel London); including quotation from 'Pledging My Time' (Bob Dylan) 5.12
3. Edward's Thrump Up 8.11
4. Blow With Ry 11.05
5. Interlude A La El Hopo; including quotation from 'The Loveliest Night Of The Year' (Webster, Ross) 2.04
6. Highland Fling (traditional, arranged Cooder, Hopkins, Watts) 4.20

The Album Track By Track

'Gimme Shelter'

Twelve months earlier, *Beggars Banquet* had opened side one with 'Sympathy for the Devil', a song that set a new benchmark for mainstream rock music with its sheer unsettling intensity. One year later, they pulled it off again by opening with a slightly shorter but equally chilling number. Although not released as a single, ever since the album appeared, it has regularly featured strongly in polls to choose the group's best songs of all time. In *Rolling Stone* magazine (appropriately, perhaps), reviewer Greil Marcus stated that it was 'a song about fear; it probably serves better than anything else as a passageway straight into the next decade. The band builds on the best melody they've ever found'. Nobody would call it catchy, but it has that indefinable spark that makes it stand out.

Richards wrote it on a miserable wet day while he was sitting in art gallery director Robert Fraser's central London apartment in Mount Street, the sky went completely black, and everybody was running for shelter from a torrential downpour. Nearly forty years later, he recalled in his memoirs, *Life*, that there was 'this incredible storm,' and he was inspired by looking out of the window 'at all these people with their umbrellas being blown out of their grasp and running like hell'. Picking up a guitar, he strummed a chord or two while improvising the opening lines, 'Ooh, a storm is threatening my very life today, If I don't get some shelter, ooh, I'm gonna fade away'. Some have read more into the lyrics than a gloomy afternoon made worse by a torrential downpour. Their theory is that Richards had been seriously worried about his relationship with Anita Pallenberg, who was co-starring with Jagger while they were shooting the movie *Performance*, in which the vocalist portrayed an eccentric, reclusive rock star. Jagger was well-known for not being one to resist temptation when handed to him on a plate, especially if the directors wanted him to shoot any intimate scenes with a female co-star. Richards insisted that he wasn't really bothered by the idea of his bandmate and girlfriend having an affair and in full view of a movie camera, but comments he made elsewhere about the film and about Jagger himself gave a different impression. Some feared for a while that it could deal a terminal blow to the

Jagger-Richards partnership and therefore, The Rolling Stones themselves.

Others listened to the lines about being threatened by flooding, or sweeping fire that 'burns like a red coal carpet, mad bull lost its way'. They suspected it had something to do with unrest engendered by the Vietnam War, a period of unease and climate of fear after a period of less than two years that had witnessed the killings of Martin Luther King, Bobby Kennedy, the 'Manson Family murders', Edward Kennedy's involvement in the accidental death of his motor passenger Mary Jo Kopechne, and above all the feeling that cultural and political upheaval was in the air. Coincidentally, John Fogerty had touched on similar lyrical territory about the same time with a hit by Creedence Clearwater Revival, released at about the same time as Richards was writing his song. Fogerty's 'Bad Moon Rising', released about the same time that 'Gimme Shelter' was being recorded, had a similarly apocalyptic scenario, with hurricanes a-blowing, rivers overflowing, and how 'the end is coming soon', but was set to such an infectious, jaunty country rock beat that its message of gloom and doom probably went over the heads of those who made it a British number one single that autumn. Jagger, who probably had no hand in its composition, agreed that 'Gimme Shelter' was 'a kind of end-of-the-world song, a very moody piece about the world closing in on you a bit. The era in which they recorded it was 'a time of war and tension', which they managed to capture to perfection.

However, he stopped short of conceding that it was about, or whether it was partly inspired by, the conflict in south-east Asia that was increasingly concentrating the minds of his generation. Speaking to *Rolling Stone* as he discussed the song a quarter of a century later, he said that 'Vietnam was not war as we knew it in the conventional sense,' not like World War Two,' but it was a particularly nasty war that people didn't want to fight'. In admitting as much, he left it to people to put their own construction on the meaning of the song.

The musical structure is remarkably simple. Richards said that it was 'Jimmy Reed inspired', with the verses on C-sharp, the intro and refrain going down C-sharp, B, A and then back up to B and C-sharp. Richards played all the guitar parts, the first few seconds of the track a distinctive, quietly ominous section where the notes seem to shimmer and are enhanced by tremolo, with Watts's subtle, beautifully concise drumming and Hopkins adding a few chords on piano, Miller's guiro on the C-sharp intro, and haunting backing vocals, before moving seamlessly into the C-sharp, B, A sequence. One commentator on a recent online thread has poetically suggested that the guitar 'screams like a vulture hovering over the dead corpse of the 60s'. Watts instantly went into a higher gear on drums while Wyman's concise bass notes, marking out the rhythm, added another dimension. The musical effect immediately created a sinister atmosphere, a smouldering, light-the-touch-paper feeling of something ominous in the air without the need for any sound effects, such as a thunderstorm or rain on a window, which would have risked sounding too gimmicky. As Richards said, 'It's got menace, all right. It's scary stuff'. His riff practically exploded into flames before Jagger's venomous yet icily controlled vocal carved out the first verse. Richards overdubbed several layers of guitars, making it difficult to emulate the original recording when they performed it onstage. The beginning of the song was so eerie, he told *Rolling Stone*, that 'sometimes in a stadium you start to hear echoes'. Yet there was a note of hope in the last verse, as the bleakness softens when we learn of refuge in a love that's 'just a kiss away'. In a world of otherwise unrelieved doom, gloom and blackness, there's light at the end of the tunnel after all.

Jagger's harmonica injected a similar note of darkness. So did the vocal of Merry Clayton, who joined him on the refrain and put heart and soul into the 'Rape, murder, it's just a shot away' section on her own after the lead break. When the band went to America in October 1969 to complete recording and mixing the album as well as go on tour, they realised that the song required a few final touches. Jagger (or perhaps Nitzsche) felt that a female vocalist ought to help out on some of the vocals. Their first choice was Bonnie Bramlett, but her husband Delaney refused to let her go and perform with the Stones, either for personal or professional reasons. One night, Botnick suggested Clayton, who had already gone to bed and was not pleased to be called out to work at such a late hour. She had never heard of The Rolling Stones, but her husband, jazz saxophonist Curtis Amy, certainly had. He knew this would do wonders for her career, and begged her not to turn the chance down. She arrived at the studio with her hair in curlers, and, despite her initial reluctance, gave a performance that really blew them all away. (Listen carefully about three minutes in on good headphones and you will hear Jagger, evidently carried away, emit a muffled 'Woo!') However, having started, she told them she wasn't going to sing any more until they had settled on her full fee. Once it was agreed, she completed it professionally in a few takes.

Her contribution would indeed make her a household name, but it came at a price. At the time, she was pregnant and later suffered a miscarriage, which she attributed to the session. Because of this, she could apparently never bear to listen to their rendition of the song, although the following year, she recorded and released a solo album on which her own version of 'Gimme Shelter' was the title track and also the single, making the lower reaches of the *Billboard* Top 100.

Part of this war cry became a nightmarish, self-fulfilling prophecy. On 6 December 1969, immediately after the release of the album, the band played the Altamont Speedway Free Festival at the end of their American tour. A member of the audience, Meredith Hunter, was high on methamphetamine during their set as he approached the front of the crowd. He tried to climb up to the stage but was stopped by the Hells Angels, who had been put in charge of security, and driven back into the crowd. Pushing his way forward again, he drew a double-barrelled long revolver from his jacket. Another of the Angels, armed with a knife and fearing he was about to shoot, stabbed him to death. He was subsequently charged with murder but acquitted on the grounds of self-defence. The title of the song gave its name to the documentary directed by Albert and David Maysles and Charlotte Zwerin, about the last weeks of the tour at the end of 1969, culminating in the events at Altamont. The song itself was a favourite of director Martin Scorsese, who used it later on the soundtrack of three of his films, *Goodfellas, Casino,* and *The Departed*.

Never released as a physical single in Britain or America, the UK Official Charts website records a two-week run as a download single only, highest position number 76, in November 2010. By then it had long since been a favourite with critics and the media. In

2012 *Ultimate Classic Rock* website chose its 100 best Rolling Stones songs and placed it at number one. Former American President Barack Obama also named it his favourite-ever track by the group.

A performance with Jagger's live vocal (including the 'rape, murder' section, some weeks before Clayton had come on the scene) sung to the pre-recorded backing track while the other four mimed on their instruments, was filmed and subsequently used in a BBC television spectacular, the 75-minute *Pop Go The Sixties*. It was shown on BBC 1 on New Year's eve 1969, and the only album track featured in a show that included several acts of the decade reprising one or two of their greatest hits. Like the live vocal and instrumental miming for 'Honky Tonk Women' as seen on *Top Of The Pops* in July and August, it had been recorded in the summer, as their clothing and the lighting screens behind them are identical and they were both done at the same time. Were the band, or Decca Records, or everyone, planning to release the track as a single and making sure there was a clip ready for television just in case? During their American tour, they also played three songs on the 23 November edition of *The Ed Sullivan Show*, namely 'Honky Tonk Women', 'Love in Vain', and 'Gimme Shelter', again with Jagger singing live while the rest mimed. Unlike the BBC, American TV was anxious to avoid anything too controversial; the 'Rape, murder' line was cut out, and surviving footage online suggests that Jagger's microphone was turned down, rendering him almost inaudible.

An alternate take with Richards on vocals, including the Clayton part, was bootlegged in the 1970s. The backing is identical to the completed version, but his voice is mixed far down and was probably intended only as a guide. Those who have seen Richards onstage with his own part-time band from the 1980s onwards, The X-Pensive Winos, will be familiar with his performance of the song. While he may not sound like a Jagger clone, he still puts the song across with that threatened feeling.

'Love In Vain'
Jagger and Richards were both part of the musical generation strongly drawn to the back catalogue of 1930s Delta bluesman Robert Johnson at a time when his recordings were almost impossible to obtain in Britain and Europe except as very expensive

imports from across the Atlantic. A year or so before they started recording *Let It Bleed*, just when they thought they knew many of his songs inside out, they discovered another collection that had been unearthed and released, including 'Love in Vain'. At the time, Richards was 'working and playing around' with Gram Parsons, an American country rock musician who was briefly a member of The Byrds and then The Flying Burrito Brothers, and between them, they decided it would be an ideal song for the Stones, but with some modification. Jagger told *Rolling Stone* that they changed the arrangement considerably. 'We put in extra chords that aren't there on the Robert Johnson version. Made it more country. And that's another strange song, because it's very poignant. Johnson was a wonderful lyric writer, and his songs are quite often about love, but they're desolate'.

The most significant chord change is the inclusion of a minor in the last line of each verse, and in the process, modifying by a small degree what had originally been basically a ballad sung and played to a 12-bar blues chord sequence. The last thing they wanted to do was destroy the integrity of the original.

The guitars are all played by Richards. A gently-picked acoustic is heard on the intro and the first line of the first verse, with some sections after that punctuated by phrases from the slide, and behind them, a gentle touch on the drums, with the bass mixed well down – on all fronts, a model of restraint. Cooder's glorious mandolin adds extra colour on the break, and continues on the third verse and final section. Until this stage, the mandolin had been almost exclusively the preserve of folk, country and bluegrass musicians. Jagger brings the emotion out well in his vocals, as he sings of following his lover with a suitcase in his hand, the last mournful parting on the station as the train arrives, and that feeling of loneliness as he looks her in the eye. This was probably as close to the roots of acoustic down-home blues as the Stones ever got. Eric Clapton also covered the song on his 2004 album *Me And Mr Johnson*, on a rather more up-tempo, full band version that combined elements of the original and the Stones' arrangement.

'Country Honk'
To those who only know this song as one of the most successful hit singles of their lengthy career, it may surprise some to find that

it was originally written in the style of country pioneers Jimmie Rodgers and Hank Williams, and heavily influenced particularly by the latter's 1951 song 'Honky Tonk Blues', a title that supplied the end of the chorus. Note – when referring to or adapting the Johnson and Williams songbooks, both the early songwriters kept to three chords; Jagger and Richards briefly introduced a fourth in the second line of the verse, and in the instrumental break. There's progress for you. The first version of the Stones' song was part of the Olympic sessions in the spring of 1969, with Richards playing all guitars, but no fiddler present. Jones may have been at the session, but was no longer contributing anything at that stage.

A few weeks later, Taylor joined, and they recorded the more familiar electric version. Richards gave their new guitarist the credit: 'And it got turned around to this other thing which got it into a completely different feel, throwing it off the wall another way'. Taylor was modest about his contribution, recalling that he 'definitely added something, but it was more or less complete by the time I arrived and did my overdubs'. Doubtless buoyed up by the massive success of the 45 that summer, they scrapped the earlier version of 'Honk' and re-recorded it in Los Angeles. This time, it included Taylor playing slide 'on one of those cheap little Selmer Hawaiian guitars, which I played on my lap in regular tuning,' and Berline on fiddle – on the pavement. Taylor used a Hawaiian lap guitar he had bought for £40 from the Selmer shop in Charing Cross Road, much beloved by major musicians of the day, apparently sold to him by a young assistant called Paul Kossoff. The lead guitarist in Free had reportedly auditioned for the Stones as well when they were looking to replace Jones, when it looked as if Free might disband after releasing their first album or at least undergo a major personnel change. Watts played drums, but bass was presumably regarded as superfluous, so there was no Wyman. There is a lyrical alteration to the first verse, which begins, 'I'm sittin' in a bar, tipplin' a jar in Jackson'. In its various forms, the song is not short of lyrical variations, as a listen to live versions on the Stones' *Get Yer Ya-Ya's Out!* and Joe Cocker's *Mad Dogs And Englishmen* the next year would show.

They felt the first version lacked something to give it that added ingredient, and Botnick recommended they should invite Byron Berline, one of the most in-demand bluegrass fiddle players on the scene, to come and add some violin. He did two takes in the studio, both of which seemed to lack something. On Johns's recommendation, they then decided to try it in the open air for some added ambience. He went out onto the pavement, wearing headphones, and one of the engineers hung a microphone with an extra-long lead out of the window to record him. In the intro, a car horn is also heard, although sources differ as to whether it was sounded by Jagger or their tour manager, Sam Cutler. (Cue mental pictures of a motorist telling the musician to get out of his way). Jagger and Richards's vocals were supplemented by those of Nanette Workman.

It is said that Gram Parsons arranged this version for the band as a quid pro quo for allowing his band The Flying Burrito Brothers to record 'Wild Horses', a Jagger-Richards composition that they began recording in December 1969 but shelved for a short time, before returning to it for the *Sticky Fingers* album.

Opinion is sharply divided among fans and critics as to its merits. Some, including this author, love and can appreciate them both for being equally effective and having their own character. Others think the Cajun-like acoustic rendition adds nothing to the song, is a misjudgement at best and downright lame, not to say dreadful, that the violin's overloud, and that it sounds like someone's singing a bit flat on the chorus. Did they really need autotune, and does it matter if someone had a drink or two (or something else) first? In online polls for the album's best and worst tracks, it often comes out rated the worst. Sean Egan, author of several books on the band and their music, agrees that Berline was a talented musician but calls his presence on this track 'whining and intrusive'. It's certainly untypical of the Stones, but with its cheerfully sloppy atmosphere, it fits in well on what was the band's most country rock album. The sound conjures up visions of a bunch of buskers plying their craft, huddled together on a pedestrian precinct in a large town or city. What it might have lacked in finesse, it gained in spontaneity and character. Of course, it was never going to be as good as the single – but how could it possibly compete against one of the most iconic rock 45s of all time?

Coincidentally, it sounds like a twin brother to 'Si Tu Dois Partir' ('If You've Gotta Go, Go Now') by Fairport Convention, recorded early in March 1969. The only British hit single by the indestructible godfathers of British folk-rock, a Bob Dylan song loosely translated into French, with Dave Swarbrick's fiddle prominent in the mix, it strikes exactly the same tone. All the Stones are missing is an accordion and a stack of chairs to knock over towards the end; all Fairport lack is the car horn. Fairport's version had been heavily played on radio that summer and peaked at number 21 in August, so it's quite likely the Stones or somebody in their circle would have heard it. Could Swarbrick's playing have been an inspiration for the addition of what would be the dominant instrument?

'Live With Me'
This marked the beginning of what would become a new pattern for the Stones' music, with saxophone becoming almost as prominent on their records as lead guitar. On the break in 'Honky Tonk Women', the saxes had been mixed well back, but this was the first track on which it came to the fore. Richards played bass, Watts brought up the rhythm section a few seconds in, and a few guitar stabs on two chords sat behind the vocals almost immediately afterwards. Wyman had become slightly detached from the Stones in the last couple of years, partly as a result of the main members' drug busts. He remained a solid, dependable musician who was never an absentee on the Brian Jones scale but sometimes stayed away from sessions, leaving the bass duties to his colleague. Piano from Russell, riding high at the time following his involvement in Joe Cocker's second major hit 'Delta Lady', helped to buttress the sound from the glissando that ushered in the first chorus onwards with his distinctively chunky chords, as did Hopkins with his more melodic touch on the keys. Bobby Keys' sax took centre stage for the break after the second chorus, and in doing so, helped to create a template for the future, one that would be enshrined in the Stones' musical lexicon for evermore when they did so again after the second verse in 'Brown Sugar', recorded later that year. After the third verse, Watts' drums built up a full head of steam as the record faded with a glorious play-out of sax and guitars competing for the audio spotlight, Taylor making his second (and final) contribution to the album on this track and

demonstrating his value with the dual lead guitar sound.

He later accurately described their recording of the track as 'kind of the start of that particular era for the Stones, where Keith and I traded licks'. Richards agreed, commenting in the 2012 documentary *Crossfire Hurricane* that, in his view, 'the real interest in playing guitar is to play guitar with another guy. Two guitars together, if you get it right, it can become like an orchestra. And Mick Taylor is a virtuoso'. Sometimes, he would refer to it as 'weaving', with both alternating on rhythm and lead guitar on the same song as the mood of the moment took them.

On many of the band's previous recordings, the vocals were often mixed down slightly and hard to work out, especially when lyrics were rarely included with an album and poor-quality medium-wave radio was the norm (although this one would surely have been banned from the airwaves). Thought-provoking lyrics were the domain of the singer-songwriter, not the rock band. Here, Jagger was well up in the mix, perhaps deliberately. Even a cursory listen makes it obvious that he was out to shock, with those horns on his head clearly visible, or else parodying himself as an absolute monster, an Aleister Crowley-like demon living a life of depravity in a grand mansion with domestic staff aplenty, all as perverted as he is. He's got nasty habits, the meat he eats for dinner must be hung up for a week, there's a score of hare-brained children locked in the nursery, the maid's a stripper, the cook's a whore, the butler has a place for her behind the pantry door, and so on. Despite this, he's trying to persuade the love of his life that there's a place for her in between the sheets, and she'd look good pram-pushing down the high street.

So what sort of dark comedy is this, and who is this reprobate? It was obviously caricature, not meant to be taken seriously, and you could almost hear him sniggering while he jotted ideas down as soon as they came into his head. To coin a phrase, 'If easily offended, stay away'. A few years later, there would probably have been a 'Parental Advisory Explicit Content' sticker on the sleeve.

'Let It Bleed'
Listen casually to the title track, and it comes across as a relaxed country, almost comfortingly folksy song. Then think about the

title and the lyrics – which, again, are quite high in the mix and clear as the proverbial bell against an unobtrusive backing – and it's obvious that Jagger's words were sailing as close to the wind as was possible in 1969 before the nation's moral guardians started foaming at the mouth. Musically, a phrase on slide guitar sounding almost like a cello supplied the first part of the intro, then some relaxed strumming on acoustic guitar was joined by drums and piano, Stewart this time – and for the only time on the album. Wyman contributed bass and autoharp, though both instruments are difficult to hear. It was taken at quite a relaxed pace, the only suggestion of any urgency being in guitar, which gradually moved up a gear towards the fade. Eagle-eyed listeners will note that at around two minutes in, at the start of the fourth verse, 'I was dreamin' of a steel guitar engagement,' that Stewart was a second behind everyone else on a piano chord change. Or was it a deliberate mistake?

Jagger's vocal, his best mock Nashville drawl, sang innocuously enough at the start about how we all need someone we can lean on. The whiff of debauchery was not far behind. By the second verse, it was getting steamy, with references to breasts being open, a space in the parking lot (use your imagination), coke and sympathy (at a time when most consumers thought the former must mean Coca Cola), needing someone to feed on, cream on, bleed on, cum on – and then a stabbing in the filthy dirty basement, not to mention a junkie nurse. Faithfull later claimed that a lot of the more sleazy references were about or else inspired by her. Almost every veiled reference to sex and drugs in the dictionary was crammed in somewhere. At the same time, it's easy to defend the lyrics about being about love, friendship, emotional dependency and suggest that the Stones were innocently reaching for comforting figures of speech. Those with a little more knowledge about the limits of slang knew otherwise with this no-holds-barred invitation for a session of unashamed lust.

The exact song title doesn't appear anywhere in the lyrics, and there are at least three possible explanations. Firstly, while they were recording the basic track in the studio, Richards was playing acoustic guitar for so long that his fingers were starting to bleed while Jagger and either Miller or one of the engineers (or both) were working on a drum track, but the guitarist was not the kind of man to let minor discomfort get in the way of his craft. While they were recording, Miller was spending a lot of time on Watts's drum sound to make sure it was just right. Nobody else noticed that Richards was in the booth, going over the slide playing and perfecting it. Eventually, he approached Miller, and said calmly but firmly that they had to finish the track that night because he couldn't play much longer. His hands, and the back of his guitar neck, were covered in blood.

'Let It Bleed, man,' was his most likely reaction to any suggestions he should take a rest. Or, once again, were they testing the limits of what they could get away with? The phrase was intravenous slang among drug users for finding a vein when the syringe plunger is pulled back and, should blood appear, letting it bleed. There is a more innocent scenario to this innuendo as well. Were Jagger and Richards, who surely had inside knowledge of what the then forthcoming Beatles LP was to be called, simply having a laugh by giving the song and then the whole album a name that was so confusingly similar, especially when the nearest the lyric came was a line about 'you can bleed on me'?

'Midnight Rambler'

After two songs about sex and drugs comes one about sex, violence, fear and murder in what the band dubbed a 'blues opera' lasting almost seven minutes in its original studio form, in live versions, anything between nine and almost 15 minutes. When they started, Richards said, 'nobody went in there with the idea of doing a blues opera, basically. Or a blues in four parts. That's just the way it turned out. I think that's the strength of the Stones or any good band. You can give them a song half raw and they'll cook it'. He saw it as a Chicago blues; 'The chord sequence isn't, but the sound is pure Chicago. I knew how the rhythm should go, it was in the tightness of the chord sequence, the D's and the A's and the E's. It wasn't a blues sequence, but it came out like heavy-duty blues'.

Lyrically, it's probably the most chilling number they ever wrote. The Beatles wrote songs about love (oh yes, and one blatant exception in the much-criticised murder tune 'Maxwell's Silver Hammer'); the Stones chose to celebrate knife-wielding maniacs.

There's a theory that it was inspired by the 'Boston Strangler', who was supposed to have killed 13 women in Boston, Mass., between 1962 and 1964; Albert DeSalvo, held in a mental institution on rape charges, confessed to the crimes in 1965, was imprisoned for life and died in 1973. Forensic experts have cast doubt on his confession, believing that evidence subsequently emerged that several killers were responsible.

Richards put paid to this, writing in *Life* that the title 'was just one of those phrases taken out of sensationalist headlines that only exist for a day. You just happen to be looking at a newspaper, "Midnight Rambler on the loose again." Oh, I'll have him'. Jagger was less specific, telling *Rolling Stone* that he and Richards wrote it together while on a holiday in Italy, but was at a loss as to why they should have written such a dark song in such idyllic surroundings. In the opening lines, Jagger teased the listener, 'Did you hear about the midnight rambler' who gave no warning but came wrapped up in a black cat coat. Later on in the song, he WAS the rambler, a maniac who was going to smash down your slate glass windows, put a first through your steel plate door – and in the final line, he'd stick his knife right down your throat.

Musically, this is just the band, with no guest keyboard players or backing vocalists. All the guitars were by Richards, standard open tuning for the main licks and then tuning all strings to the chord of E for the slide. When it was recorded, Jones was nominally still a band member and is credited as playing percussion, possibly as a parting gift. If he really was, he must have been so far down in the mix as to be well nigh inaudible. The Englishman whose love of vintage American blues had inspired so many of his fellow countrymen to retune their guitars so they could play bottleneck-style was no longer needed. At the mic, it was Jagger playing out the part of a maniac as he sang, teased, sneered, screamed and growled, adding harmonica as a foil to Richards's razor-sharp guitars, all buttressed by Wyman and Watts on the rhythm section. It opened as a kind of blues shuffle, breaking into a jerky start-stop routine and a brief stop altogether. A slow, dramatic section took over, with sparse guitar and spooky harmonica sounds, before the pace quickened with drums for the final blood-curdling finish.

This was the third song in a row that apparently made members of the London Bach Choir decide they didn't want their hallowed name besmirched by connection with such a record, hence the black bar that obliterated their name on the inner bag credits. Assuming they received complimentary copies on release, they can't have been thrilled by what came out of their stereos. There was no avoiding the fact that, on an album with a generous diet of sleaze and unashamed devilry, this probably tops what would once have been known as the X-certificate list. Although it became a highlight of their live shows for some years, a more mature Jagger, a father, grandfather and great-grandfather to several girls, would freely admit that he could never imagine himself writing such a song again.

'You Got The Silver'

After a trilogy of sex, drugs and violence, the album reverted to a semi-Nashville twang with the theme of good old-fashioned romance. When asked what it was about, Richards once joked that he just loved singing about precious metal, and by that, he didn't mean heavy metal; 'I always try and capture feelings rather than explain things'. The sub-text was 'from Keith to Anita', rather in the manner of John Lennon laying bare his love for Yoko, or Paul McCartney for Linda. Where Jagger came straight to the point and said there was a place for him and his loved (or lusted-after) one between the sheets, Richards went for the more gentlemanly minstrel approach; 'Tell me, honey, what will I do, when I'm hungry and thirsty too, feeling foolish and that's for sure, Just waiting here at your kitchen door?' He's clearly singing his heart out; 'Oh babe, you got my soul / You got the silver, you got the gold / If that's your love, it just made me blind / I don't care, no, that's no big surprise'.

The melody is very simple, never straying from the time-honoured three chords of E, A and B, played by Richards on his Gibson Hummingbird guitar, strings tuned to the chord of E. This could almost be a Dylan love song from his *Nashville Skyline* phase or even a number from one of Rod Stewart's early solo albums. There's a common theme in that Richards accompanied himself mostly on acoustic slide guitar with a little backwards echo in places, tuned to the chord of E. It was an arrangement pretty close to some of Stewart's mainly acoustic love songs, accompanied on slide by Ron Wood, the man who later replaced Taylor, who had filled the space alongside Richards vacated by Jones.

There were a few stabs of electric guitar from near the end of the first verse onwards. Just over a minute in, Hopkins's Hammond organ swirled into the mix to sweeten the flavour and add something to the acoustic guitar. Jones was credited on autoharp, his contribution being used on the instrumental break, but was again evidently well down in the mix (like his percussion on the previous track) and can barely be heard. Only in the final minute or so, on the last two verses, did Richards drive everything up a gear or two on vocals and guitars. Meanwhile, Watts, who used brushes on his drums for the first part of the song, now matched him by using his sticks almost until the final notes, and Hopkins's piano overdub added to the flavour as well. Wyman's bass was almost inaudible.

An earlier version, presumably featuring the same backing track as the instruments all sounded nearly identical, had Jagger on vocal – and Jones's autoharp higher in the mix. There was very little to choose between both versions, and Jagger gave the same emphasis to each line. Richards' voice on the finished version was a little huskier, but to use his own phrase, 'spreading the workload' was only fair, as was the matter of him being allowed to sing such a personal lyric that he had created himself. Jagger's version must have reinforced doubts regarding the truth of Johns' confession about accidentally wiping the lead singer's contribution while he was on his movie star *alter ego* at the other end of the universe. But its writer was truly very much in love, evidently angry and helpless at the Jagger-Pallenberg fling. Moreover, the story about Richards having blood on his hands and the neck of the guitar after an intensive recording session has been mentioned with reference to the title track. If it did happen on both songs, the battle-scarred guitarist had certainly earned his right to do so on this one. Jagger's version, by the way, has Jones's contribution on autoharp more audible. Some say that the slide guitar may have been by Ry Cooder; if not, Richards was surely inspired by his style of playing.

His laid-back singing gave the whole song a different colour, which it would have lacked had it been another Jagger vocal.

Until the album's release, everyone just thought of Richards as the guitarist and the man who just stepped up to the mic to add backing vocals on stage every time some rough harmonies were needed on a chorus. He had previously sung lead only on 'Connection', a song on *Between The Buttons*, one of their less-heralded tracks. His relaxed yet lovelorn crooning on this slow burner really raised his profile as one of the gentlest, most straightforward songs on an album on which almost every other song was keen to grab the listener by the jugular. To teenagers who loved the Stones as a band who rocked yet still sounded commercial, this and 'Love in Vain' sounded on the first few listens, either maudlin or boring. With time, they both stood revealed as beautifully crafted jewels, placed perfectly on both sides between more typical fare.

'Monkey Man'

The penultimate track seems to be the album's least talked-about number, a groove rather than a song. While there's no doubting its merits, it's a little lacking in that extra 'wow' factor. Every other track has some kind of notoriety, sparkle or extra twist, that sets the bar so very high. This does catch fire, but not to the same extent. It is, however, quite unlike anything else on the record, and helps to break new ground for them – as do most, if not all, of the other eight cuts.

Here was one of those songs that probably came about more or less spontaneously, through jamming in rehearsals. Hopkins kick-started it with the opening piano riff, Richards took it further with a few spontaneously created ideas on guitar, and Jagger came up with the lyrics, a playful poke at their bad-boys public image, while as ever, Wyman and Watts supplied the rhythm. The rhymes may be pretty contrived – 'pizza' and 'squeezer' weren't exactly their finest moment, but it hardly mattered.

Richards was responsible for all the guitars. Musically, it was built around fairly basic chords, with an intro of C-sharp, B and A on the guitar, underpinned by Wyman's simple bass plus deceptively sweet touches on the vibes and a steady rhythm from the tambourine before Watts' drums entered. It was also the start of their funk phase (or should it be 'jazz-funk'?), a genre they would revisit with subsequent cuts in the next decade like 'Can't

You Hear Me Knocking', and disco-era cuts like 'Hot Stuff' and 'Hey Negrita', which again evolved through jamming sessions. Though Jagger's part-sung, part-declaimed vocals took centre stage as ever, Richards' guitars were the star of the show. Wood later called the riff his favourite Keith riff of all time. Most of it consisted of razor-sharp variations on the most basic of phrases imaginable, punctuated with little licks on slide, plus more melodic touches from Hopkins' piano. For about fifty seconds, the song was largely a showcase for guitar, in the key of C-sharp, until some sweeping piano on an E B A B phrase played four times added an elegantly melodic touch, only to be swept away for the final minute or so as Jagger's increasingly frenzied screaming of 'I'm a monkey!', returning to C-sharp, pulled it kicking for dear life towards the fade.

Maybe they were rarely asked because journalists thought the meanings were too obvious, but the band made little if any reference to it in interviews, thus allowing fans and commentators to have let their imaginations run riot as to what the song means. Jagger was being described by the press as looking like a monkey, and was poking fun at himself and his public image – 'I'm a fleabit peanut monkey [a person with a sexually transmitted disease], and all my friends are junkies'. Yes, they were sex-crazed devil-worshippers if you wanted them to live up to their image in the tabloid press. They could laugh at themselves as well. Drugs had to come into it, naturally, and 'having a monkey on your back' was slang for heroin addiction. 'Monkey' and 'junkie' made an obvious rhyming couplet, and it can be a mistake to over-analyse lyrics that were made up in the studio to fit as piece of music that presumably started as a jamming session. Add to this the theories about how Jagger sang 'I hope we're not too messianic, or a trifle too satanic, we just love to play the blues,' reportedly a comment on whether he was questioning his personal beliefs and wondering if he has gone too far in his setting himself up as a spokesman for the counter-culture or the 'permissive society' and quest for personal liberation. All he wanted to do was play his music.

Or was it just colossal self-parody from the crown prince of the bad boys in rock 'n' roll, living up to their public image and taunting the more conservative views of middle England, as he did on 'Live With Me'? The monkey man could also be a tongue-in-cheek commentary to suggest someone who wanted to break free from human constraints and civilisation to go and live a life of freedom. Ray Davies would express the same ideas a year later in 'Apeman', The Kinks' last British top five hit, when he sang of not feeling safe in the world any more, not wanting to die in a nuclear war, and sail away to a distant shore where he could live like an apeman. But despite the serious underlying message, Davies sang it all with a grin on his face. So did Jagger with 'Monkey Man'.

'We just love to play the blues'. In the 1960s, racism and a degree of segregation were endemic to a degree that seems almost beyond belief in the 21st century. It was largely their passion for the Delta blues that created The Rolling Stones in the first place, at a time when pop and rock 'n' roll was largely the white man's domain, as performed by Elvis Presley, Cliff Richard, Buddy Holly, then followed by The Beatles and The Beach Boys. But none of these acts could resist the spell of Chuck Berry, Fats Domino, Muddy Waters and Tamla Motown. The Stones were proud to hang out with the latter at a time when black music was struggling to enter the mainstream, particularly in Britain. African-Americans and taunts of 'monkey' in particular were the butt of negative if not downright racist comments and slurs from the white community, and the Stones revelled in making a stand on their behalf. If Jagger was a monkey man, it was a badge he wore with unashamed defiance.

The 'monkey man', it is believed, was not the vocalist but Mario Schifano, an Italian post-modernist painter, collagist and occasional film director. He hung out with the Stones for part of the 1960s, and had brief affairs with Anita Pallenberg and Marianne Faithfull at various times. The reference to a 'cold Italian pizza' is thought to be him, and also a name for decadence, especially as Schifano and some of his girlfriends were well-known drug users. As for the 'lemon squeezer', this was a sexual euphemism taken from Robert Johnson's 'Travelling Riverside Blues'. Cock rock had been around since before Jagger was even born. Almost any of the phrases in the lyrics, like mentions of 'lemon squeezer' (sex or drugs?), can be interpreted to mean anything the listener would like them to mean. The line 'I was bitten by a boar, I was gouged and I was gored, But I pulled on through' might be seen as a metaphor for surviving the hard times, like the line in 'Jumpin' Jack Flash' about being drowned, washed up and left for dead. This has tempted some to see it as an expression of 'survival of the fittest' and link it with Darwinian evolutionary theory as a way of describing the survival of the fittest. It would take a book in itself to dissect the lyrics line by line and link them with all the different interpretations put on everything.

'You Can't Always Get What You Want'

It's also now noticeable that a pattern has emerged, a common bond between *Beggars Banquet* and *Let It Bleed*. Side one on both albums starts with a dark, sinister piece, followed by a poignant, slide guitar-driven blues song, then a country number. Turn over to side two for a tale of violence, whether it's about people fighting in the streets or a knife-wielding maniac terrorising the local population at midnight, then followed by another subdued blues meets country item. To end the journey was a song that started with a choral section, then became a plaintive acoustic folk ballad, morphed into gospel-meets-funk, and then simply soared, pushed along by guest keyboard players, Richards's guitar licks, backing singers in unison and the reappearance of the choir. To quote Jagger, whose song it clearly was, speaking to Jann Wenner of *Rolling Stone*, 'It's a kind of end-of-the-world song, really. It's apocalypse; the whole record's like that. It's a very rough, very violent era. The Vietnam War. Violence on the screens. Pillage and burning'.

The select few who had been invited to the recording of the still not publicly screened *Rock And Roll Circus* saw and heard the song's premiere on stage, a shortened run-through that gave only a taster of what it would develop into, and purchasers of 'Honky Tonk Women' had heard an edit lasting 4.42 that omitted the choral intro and a verse but at least included the finale. In discussions that summer about what was to be the A-side of their forthcoming single, Johns had stated the case for this track to be made the one. The singer disagreed, and the others were on his side. Eric Clapton, who was working in the next-door studio, was invited to listen to both tracks and give his opinion. He looked coldly at Johns, told him he was mad, and said it had to be 'Honky Tonk Women'.

Those who might have agreed with Johns, and there must have been more than a few, could at last revel in what was immediately recognised as one of rock music's masterpieces, once they heard the full, unedited version on album. Enter the London Bach Choir with the a capella first verse and chorus. Fifty seconds later came a lone acoustic guitar on the chords of C and F, a few flourishes of French horn, followed by Jagger's first verse and chorus with percussion and organ joining in, drums and backing vocals bursting forth on the last line. From there, the whole song took flight until the end. Piano joined in on the third verse, with a short bridge on the chords of D-min, A-min, F, D-min and G (in contrast to the verses which stayed on C and F throughout and added a solitary D in the chorus. An impassioned scream from Jagger led into a wordless section from the chorus, bookended by a reprise of the bridge with piano, organ and drums, and another verse. At the final 'get what you need' on the chorus, the choir appeared for the remainder of the song, almost two minutes until the fade, with piano and drums leading the backing. Thirty seconds from the end, the chorus rose ever higher, and the beat changed from its gospel shuffle to double-time drumming for the final section.

The choir members were brought in initially to add harmonies to the end section and create a coda reminiscent of the long 'la la la' singalong fadeout on The Beatles' 'Hey Jude', as Jagger had admired the lengthy coda on that but wanted to try and go one better. They did, for the Stones' song would boast a much more ambitiously-crafted arrangement than the Fab Four's straightforward song culminating in four minutes of the closing 'Na-na-na na' phrase and title repeated to fadeout.

As for the lyrics, there was evidently a slice or two of the frontman's memoirs to be gleaned from the verses. Marianne Faithfull asserted that she was the female character in the first verse whom he saw at the reception with a glass of wine in her hand and a footloose man at her feet. She admitted she was being used as a muse for this and at least one of the group's other songs, but all the same, conceded it was 'a worthy cause'. Next, he told of his day out in the summer of 1968 when taking part with thousands of others in a demonstration in central London against the Vietnam War. An extended verse dwelt on his visit to the Chelsea Drugstore, a pub in Kings Road, London, and the mysterious Mr Jimmy. According to who you choose to believe, this could have been either producer Jimmy Miller or possibly Jimi Hendrix, whose glorious but short career as rock music's most innovative guitarist was now in freefall. Or was it a different person entirely – Jimmy Hutmaker, a local character in Excelsior, Minnesota, whom Jagger had met a few years before when queueing up unsuccessfully in a drugstore for a Cherry Cola? As he turned to leave, Hutmaker muttered to him the phrase that would give birth to the song. The narrative turns full circle with the last verse, as Marianne Faithfull (assuming it is her) stands once again at the reception, with the slightly surrealist image of bloodstained hands holding a glass with a bleeding man inside.

On the face of it, the verses painted a bleak, disjointed tale. There was a vague sense of half-hearted optimism in the title, which could be construed in other words as a resigned 'don't expect too much, and maybe you'll get by'. Jagger was proud of what he had achieved in the song, commenting that people could identify with it; nobody ever gets what they always want, settling for second-best is all you can expect. It had all the ingredients, namely a singalong chorus, a good melody, and very good arrangements.

Close to half a century later, it would cast something of a spell, particularly in the political arena, on both sides of the Atlantic. In 2016, American Presidential candidate Donald Trump played the Rolling Stones' recording of the song at campaign appearances during the republican primaries and the election itself. Although his campaign managers had a licence from ASCAP, the band had no time whatsoever for Trump, made it clear that they didn't endorse his campaign and asked him to stop forthwith, but he ignored them. He continued to use it when campaigning unsuccessfully for a second term in 2020. Meanwhile, in England, Labour Member of Parliament Jo Cox was attacked and murdered while on constituency business in June 2016. A new version of the song was recorded later that year and credited to Friends of Jo Cox, featuring MP4, an all-party quartet of musician MPs, and others, including Steve Harley, Ricky Wilson, David Gray and K.T. Tunstall. It was released as a download-only single, a few promo CDs were also made available to the media, and proceeds donated to a charity set up in Cox's name, although it failed to reach the Top 100.

'Gimme Shelter' was an astonishingly potent overture to the album, and 'You Can't Always Get What You Want' an equally impressive conclusion. In a sense, it was the Stones' 'Bohemian Rhapsody' – an epic, a supremely ambitious, carefully crafted piece of work that the band produced only a few years into their career. Although they stayed together for many years afterwards, perhaps far longer than they, their fans or even their detractors could ever have predicted, it set the bar so high that they could find it hard to surpass in one individual track what Jagger would later refer to self-deprecatingly as 'a sort of doomy ballad about drugs in Chelsea'.

Reception And Commercial Performance

When *Beggars Banquet* entered the shops in December 1968, reviews were uniformly ecstatic. One year earlier, it had been the turn of the marmite *Their Satanic Majesties* Request, an imaginative but rather too hippy-trippy departure into ersatz psychedelia regarded at the time as a misstep, although its reputation has since recovered. (Interestingly, both peaked at number three in Britain). This time, high expectations were amply fulfilled with what was instantly recognisable as their best long-player yet. The band then rode out the storm of losing their founding member turned major liability and acquired a much younger, as yet little-known guitarist who had yet to prove himself. After that, they returned to live work, in the wake of 'Honky Tonk Women' that was at the time, with five weeks at the top in Britain and four in America, and would remain probably their most successful single ever. Nobody was disappointed, and five months later critics were falling over themselves again to find the right superlatives for *Let It Bleed*. Maybe they were looking for 'the' album that would become some kind of artistic, musical landmark to define the end of the 1960s in style. Bob Dylan's most recent, *Nashville Skyline*, had been a pleasant but undemanding country album (yes, another country rock album, but it didn't exactly rock) that delighted some fans but disappointed others, while The Beatles' *Abbey Road* lived up to expectations but was released to a backdrop of growing suspicions (soon to be confirmed) that the quartet were about to pull the plug on their collective partnership for good. In contrast, their freshly-recharged rivals had just roared back with what might just be their best collection on vinyl yet. There was also a certain irony in that *Abbey Road*, after having hugged the number one spot in the British album charts ever since release in September 1969, should be displaced by *Let It Bleed*, albeit for only one week. In its home country, it went platinum with sales of 300,000, while in the US, it peaked at number three, and went double platinum with sales of 2,000,000.

Greil Marcus, writing in *Rolling Stone*, compared it and *Beggars Banquet* to *Highway 61 Revisited*, often regarded as Bob Dylan's best. He had words of praise for almost every track, from the 'brilliant revival' of 'Love in Vain' and the 'haunting ride through the diamond mines' of 'You Got the Silver', to the 'bravado' of

'Midnight Rambler' and 'Live With Me'. Special accolades were reserved for the opening and closing tracks, the two that seemed to matter most; 'both reach for reality and end up confronting it, almost mastering what's real, or what reality will feel like as the years fade in'. He was less complimentary about the sleeve design, which had 'the crummiest cover art since *Flowers'* (a 1967 US-only compilation) and a list of credits inside that looked like it had been designed by the US Government Printing Office. Other reviews were equally favourable about the music, if less prescient, less articulate about the sense of doom it foresaw or presented about a world that was losing its sense of direction as the decade came to an end. In Britain, a very enthusiastic if rather pedestrian appraisal in *New Musical Express* by Richard Green said there was 'so much variety that each track makes you want to hear it again and again'.

Throughout the years, the record's reputation grew in stature. It soon became a given that it was number two in the four-album run of undisputed classic album releases by the band, the best they ever made. Retrospective polls compiled some years later, whether voted for by music fans and readers of the rock press or industry insiders, had no hesitation in placing it high. Some thirty years later, Stephen Davis, one of the band's biographers, opined that 'No rock record, before or since, has ever so completely captured the sense of palpable dread that hung over its era'. On the fiftieth anniversary of its release, Rob Sheffield wrote in *Rolling Stone* that the album sounded more timely than ever, calling it 'a masterpiece that holds up as the ultimate rock & roll album for bleak times' as well as their darkest album, yet also their funniest — and above all their greatest.

Every classic album has its flaws, not to mention a rock critic or two ready to point them out. Richie Unterberger, in *All Music Guide To Rock,* contends that the Stones were never as consistent on album as The Beatles. *Let It Bleed*, he opined, 'suffers from some rather perfunctory tracks', like 'Country Honk' and 'Monkey Man', but agreed that 'Gimme Shelter' and what he called 'the stunning' 'You Can't Always Get What You Want' are among their very best, as well as singling out 'You Got the Silver' and 'Love in Vain' which he found 'as close to the roots of acoustic down-home blues as the Stones ever got'.

Let It Bleed, Deja Que Sangre (Mexico), or *Déjalo Sangrar* (Argentina) has been issued and reissued in several formats and variations on the Decca, London and ABKCO labels over its half-century and counting. In addition to the usual CDs and cassettes, for those with deep pockets, there have been picture discs, official and unofficial, and coloured vinyl (red, naturally, and also hand-poured red and black together). The most enticing is a 50th anniversary limited edition of 27,000 copies, a joint production including the stereo blue label 180g vinyl and remastered SACD on London, the mono red label 180g vinyl and remastered SACD on Decca, the 7" 'Honky Tonk Women' 45 in mono on London with replica picture sleeve, in a hand-numbered box including 80-page illustrated hardcover book, three hand-numbered replica lithographs, and a replica of the original poster.

Live Performances, Variations And Re-Recorded Versions

Apart from 'Country Honk', which was never played live for obvious reasons (no 'Unplugged Rolling Stones' with fiddles, then, *à la* Status Quo's *Aquostic*), all the songs on the album have regularly been featured on stage, sometimes enhanced with the appearance of a well-known guest artiste or two. What performer, be he or she ever so big, could ever turn down a chance to share the spotlight with Mick Jagger in front of hundreds or more for a few minutes? It is a testament to the fact that even most of the less well-known songs are still well-remembered and loved by audiences almost as much as the oldies that were hits in the 1960s and 1970s. In most cases they are a little longer than their recorded counterparts, allowing room for a degree of improvisation and audience participation. The only official live sets not to feature any tracks from the album are *Still Life* (1982) and *El Mocambo 1977* (2022).

'Gimme Shelter'

'Gimme Shelter' appeared in the set lists for most of the 1969 American tour that coincided with the album release. Although some critics maintain that the recorded version has been hard, if not impossible, to match, it has remained a regular fixture in their set lists from the 1972 American tour onwards, embellished in recent years with guest performers, up to the No Filter Tour of 2017-21, on which several dates were postponed because of Jagger and Watts's health problems, and then because of the COVID-19 pandemic. On Wyman's departure in 1993, Darryl Jones joined on bass as a touring (but not full) member. The gigs resumed in 2021 with Steve Jordan, who had played with Richards in the X-Pensive Winos, replacing Watts on drums; the latter was seriously ill and died in August, aged 80, shortly before the last dates were played. Perhaps the finest of the lot, certainly the most star-studded, was one played at the Rock and Roll Hall of Fame benefit concert at Madison Square Gardens in October 2009, by U2 with Bono, Jagger and Fergie all sharing vocals, separately and together, plus will.i.am on piano and synthesiser. From 1989 to 2015, the Stones' backing vocalist on live shows was Lisa Fischer, her place being taken after that by Sasha Allen. During their 2012 50th anniversary tour, the Merry Clayton role was handled at various gigs by Mary J. Blige, Florence Welch, and Lady Gaga, sometimes taking the lead in verses and trading lines with Jagger. In recent years performances have been stretched out to greater length by an extended intro, coda and extra instrumental passages between verses, often reaching and even going past the seven-minute mark.

Additionally, it has been covered by over 100 other artists, sometimes for good causes. In 1993, the British Food Records label commissioned certain acts, in some cases combinations of two artists, to record the song in different genres to raise funds for the Shelter charity's 'Putting Our House in Order' project. Issued on various formats including CD and cassette single, and 12" vinyl 45, they included 'pop versions' (Voice of the Beehive and Jimmy Somerville, Heaven 17 with Hannah Jones and a live version by the Stones themselves); 'alternative versions' (New Model Army and Tom Jones, Cud and Sandie Shaw, Kingmaker); 'rock versions' (Thunder, Little Angels, and the odd coupling of Hawkwind with Samantha Fox); and even 'dance versions' (808 State and Robert Owens, Pop Will Eat Itself vs Gary Clail vs Ranking Roger vs The Mighty Diamonds vs The On U Sound System). There's nothing like being spoilt for choice, but to these ears, Thunder and Little Angels acquit themselves better than the rest, though Jones's take with the Army featuring Nine Below Zero's Mark Feltham on harmonica runs them close. For the Official Charts Company's Top 100, sales of all versions were counted together as a Various Artists EP. It entered at its highest position, number 23, staying on the list for four weeks, with BBC1's *Top Of The Pops* playing Voice of the Beehive and Somerville in the first week.

In addition to Merry Clayton's recording mentioned above, as a single and the title track of her 1970 album, Grand Funk Railroad included a version on their album *Survival* in 1971, and as a single, it reached number 61 on the US *Billboard* chart. Paolo Nutini covered the song as a bonus track on his CD single 'Coming Up Easy', in 2009, and as a result, was asked by Mick Jagger and Ben Affleck to perform the track for a documentary of the same name on the plight of the millions of people displaced from their homes as a result of fighting in the Sudanese region. At the last count, over a hundred artists have recorded the song, among them Inspiral Carpets, Paul Brady and The Forest Rangers, Sisters of Mercy and The Patti Smith Group, while Meat Loaf occasionally performed it on stage.

Live albums and movies: *No Security* (1998); *Live Licks* (2004); *Ladies And Gentlemen: The Rolling Stones* (1974 concert movie, released DVD, Blu-ray, 2010); *Hyde Park Live* (2013*)*; *Brussels Affair* (1973, released 2011); *Totally Stripped* (2016, 2-disc edition); *Havana Moon* (2016 concert movie, DVD + CD), *Grrr Live!* (2012, released 2023)

'Love In Vain'
This was one of the two songs from the album to be given its premiere at the July 1969 Hyde Park show. Taylor played slide guitar while Richards added lead on standard tuning, on a rather rough and ready performance that gave no inkling of the delicate beauty that lay in store. It was included on their American tour to promote *Exile On Main St* in June 1972, again with Taylor on slide, and made it to *Ladies And Gentlemen* but was rested after that until revived in a semi-acoustic version on *Stripped* over twenty years later. The slide guitar duties then devolved on Ronnie Wood, and this time, they turned in a far better version, even despite a false start when they had to play it again after the beginning of the first verse.
Live albums and movies: *Stripped* (1995); *Ladies And Gentlemen: The Rolling Stones.*

'Live With Me'
This was the first of the two songs on the album to receive a first public airing on *Get Yer Ya-Ya's Out!* This time Richards and Taylor both played lead guitar, as they did on the record, and the intro features lead as well instead of bass on its own for the opening bars. They tore through it at a cracking pace, completing it in three minutes flat and ending on the final chorus, though sounding a little loose with Jagger's vocals mixed back, and without any piano or saxes. Stewart played piano on the live album, but only on three non-*Let It Bleed* songs. The 1969 American tour was notable for being their last on which they

appeared without backing vocalists or additional musicians (if we still include 'Stu' as the sixth Stone).

By the time it appeared on another live album, *No Security*, eighteen years later, the Stones' touring personnel had expanded considerably so they could reproduce their more ambitious arrangements better onstage. This time, the bass in the intro only lasts for a bar or so before being joined by lead guitar, while new regular keyboard player Chuck Leavell provided the appropriate flourishes, plus two sax players (one being Bobby Keys, who played on the original), and although there's no confirmation that they appeared on this number as well, the album credits also listed other players on trumpet and trombone.

Yet another live version, and arguably the best, was from a show from the Beacon Theatre, New York City, November 2006. Featuring Jagger trading lines from each verse with a feisty Christina Aguilera and both of them sharing the chorus, it appeared on *Shine A Light*, a single CD, double CD and concert film directed by Martin Scorsese.

The highest-profile cover version was by Girlschool, Britain's best-known female heavy metal band of their time. Slightly faster than the original, and with lead guitar instead of sax, it appeared on their Top 30 album *Screaming Blue Murder* (1982). West country indie band The Crowmen also recorded it on the B-side of a single, 'She Makes Me Ill' in 1991, on their only release to date, again with guitars but no sax. Sheryl Crow has performed the song several times on stage, sometimes coming on as a guest with the Stones and duetting with Jagger, or with her own band, playing harmonica where the sax break was on the original, with her own band on TV, and at a Farm Aid benefit in New Carolina in 2022. Her autobiographical documentary *Sheryl* and the accompanying soundtrack CD that same year also included her own version, with Jagger playing harmonica.

Live albums and movies: *Get Yer Ya-Ya's Out!*; *No Security* (1998); *Shine A Light* (2008); *Ladies And Gentlemen: The Rolling Stones*; *Totally Stripped* (5-disc limited edition, 2016)

'Let It Bleed'

The title track was passed over in the repertoire for some twelve years, until it became a regular item on the 1981-82 American tour. Bobby Keys added a sax break, while Jagger played acoustic guitar (usually 6-string but sometimes 12-string), Richards lead and Wood slide, as they did on all subsequent performances. After that, it disappeared until the mid-nineties, on a few dates in 1995 during the Voodoo Lounge tour. A live recording from a club show at L'Olympia Bruno Coquatrix, Paris that June, about a minute shorter than the studio version, appeared on *Stripped*, with Jagger doing his best mock-country drawl, and Leavell on keyboards.

It was brought back for a few dates on the protracted No Filter tour, with neither piano nor saxophone. Cover versions were recorded by Johnny Winter on *Still Alive And Well* in 1973, and as the B-side of a single by Joan Jett and The Blackhearts in 1990. Live album: *Stripped* (1995)

'Midnight Rambler'

The second of two *Let It Bleed* songs to take a bow in Hyde Park before the record was completed, it became another regular live staple, and indeed a showstopper. While they were preparing for the American tour that autumn, their lighting director, Chip Monck, devised a custom light rig, a genuine first as far as rock bands were concerned. It was used to great effect on this number, with red lights shining on Jagger at a particular time to enhance the dramatic effect. The performance on *Get Yer Ya-Ya's Out!* was extended from just under seven minutes to over nine, allowing for a longer intro with extra harmonica, and a point 4½ minutes in where the music slowed down, came to a brief stop, apart from a few guitar sounds – and the audience, who had obviously had no opportunity to hear the song before seeing it onstage, dutifully applauded as they assumed it was the end. A few guitar phrases built up to the vocalist's measured, theatrically drawn-out, 'Well you heard about the Boston' [cue cavernous thump on drums] and the gradual climb back to a slow blues, with some more improvisation on the way. For the last ninety seconds or so, it accelerated back to the same temp at which it started, paving the way for that chilling, closing, 'I'll stick my knife right down your throat, baby, and it HURTS!' It sounded just that little more free-flowing than the studio version, but again it was improved with a little help from studio technology.

One reason *Get Yer Ya-Ya's Out!* was released was to beat the boot-leggers, responsible for unleashing a much-in-demand rival recording Live-r Than You'll Ever Be, featuring material from one of their shows at Oakland Coliseum on 9 November 1969 and 'released' about a month later. It would obviously never pay them anything in royalties. Decca's legitimate release had to be better, and a certain amount of doctoring went on with the moving of spoken intros from the stage, Jagger patching up and even replacing some vocals, and Richards improving his ragged vocal harmonies sung under the influence that weren't audible to equally high concertgoers caught up in the heat of the moment, but would have sounded decidedly below par on that state-of-the-art turntable and stereo speakers in the home living room.

Their frontman honed his stage performance of the number over time, entering into the spirit of the occasion as he declaimed the vocals, crawling around, lashing the stage with his belt. After Taylor left the band in 1974 and they resumed touring with Ronnie Wood on guitar, the song became even longer, often stretching to almost 15 minutes.

It was temporarily retired from the repertoire when the band went on hiatus for a while. By the mid-1980s Jagger seemed intent on launching himself as a soloist, Britain's answer to Michael Jackson, much to Richards' fury. For a time, it looked as if it might be the end, but it turned out to be a sabbatical while each member attended to business elsewhere. Even the lead guitarist, deciding that if you can't beat 'em, join 'em, also formed his own band and released a solo album. The 1980s ended with them back where they belonged, both main members still sparring, writing and recording together, touring and revisiting their old repertoire with what seemed like renewed enthusiasm. With the intervals between each new studio album becoming longer and longer, there were less new greatest hits to replace the tried and tested classics, and 'Midnight Rambler' was dusted down for the select series of smaller venue concerts in 1995, a performance at Brixton Academy in July appearing on *Totally Stripped*, plus more in the 21st century when it was again a regular part of the setlist. Taylor rejoined the band as a special guest on the 50 & Counting Tour, joining them on stage for a 12-minute version.

It's difficult to imagine other acts flocking to bring us their own version of this song. One of the few to do so was American blues singer and guitarist Larry McCray in 1997, lasting just over four minutes, in a more funky rhythm than the blues shuffle that powers most of the original and sounding rather like B.B. King, nearly half of it taken up with a lead guitar and organ break. There are also instrumentals by sax player Robin Morris, on a Rolling Stones tribute album, *Play It Loud* (2011), which also included a similar treatment of 'Gimme Shelter', and one by a bluegrass duo, Dennis Caplinger and Sharon Whyte. Needless to say, none of these are anything like as chilling as the original.

Live albums and movies: *Get Yer Ya-Ya's Out!*; *Ladies And Gentlemen: The Rolling Stones*; *Hyde Park Live* (2013); *Totally Stripped* (2-disc edition, 2016); *Havana Moon*; *Brussels Affair*; *Grrr Live!*

'You Got The Silver'

For many years, this was a curiously neglected number. It was played on stage for the first time during the No Security Tour in 1999, and at once became a regular on the setlist, reappearing on the A Bigger Bang Tour from 2005 to 2007. At first, Richards was surprised at how well the song they had almost forgotten was going down live and how everyone sang along. Wood said he never knew how much people really liked it, and he himself took the credit for bringing it back into the repertoire. A live performance from November 2006 appeared on the *Shine A Light* film and soundtrack album.

It came back for the 50 and Counting tour of 2012-13, which included a finale of two shows at Hyde Park, and on the No Filter Tour. On live performances, Richards and Wood took centre stage, both with amplified acoustic guitars, Wood playing slide and Richards adding occasional chords but for most of the song concentrating on vocal, while Watts again played brushes on his drumkit until the final section.

The song was also covered by Susan Tedeschi on her album *Hope And Desire* (2005), and by Cat Power as a bonus track on *Covers* (2022), both closely following the original.

Live albums and movies: *Shine A Light*; *Ladies And Gentlemen: The Rolling Stones*; *Havana Moon*; *Hyde Park Live*

'Monkey Man'

As befitted what was arguably the least musically interesting track on the album – and that's no criticism, for the competition from the rest was pretty intense – this was also on the 'in abeyance' list for a long time. It seems to have been absent from the repertoire until the 2002-3 world tour, which provided material for *Live Licks*. One assumes that it was brought back at the request of Wood, who had always liked it. Being a fairly short song built around Richards's riffing in C-sharp and then the rather more tuneful E B A B sequence, it's partly a showcase for both guitarists to have a well-controlled jam that results in a performance about half a minute shorter than the original. It fell to Chuck Leavell, a regular 'additional Rolling Stone' on tour and record since 1981, to reprise the role of Nicky Hopkins, who had died in 1995 after a long battle with Crohn's Disease, on keyboards.

In the cover versions of *Let It Bleed* numbers league table, it also comes at the bottom of the list, with only five recorded so far. The main one to look out for was by Onionhead, a Birmingham-based indie rock band, on a 3-track 12" EP *Electric Ladland* (1990).
Live albums: *Live Licks* (2004)

'You Can't Always Get What You Want'

A cursory listen to the first live performance on *Rock And Roll Circus* and then the full album version makes it apparent that the song was very much a studio creation, and that it would take more than a five-piece rock band to do it justice on stage. Its first TV appearance, alongside 'Honky Tonk Women', was on *The David Frost Show* in June 1969, with the customary live lead vocal and backing track from both sides of the record, including the choir on this one. It was regularly performed live from the summer 1972 American tour onwards, with Nicky Hopkins on piano. The June 1976 performance from Les Abattoirs, Paris, on *Love You Live*, with Ian Stewart and Billy Preston credited as keyboard players, had a rather plaintive, almost watery synthesiser sound (reminiscent of the one they achieved on their 1976 Top 10 hit 'Fool to Cry') on the intro, vainly trying to compensate for the lack of French horn, plenty of unexceptional soloing and audience singing alone – really for completists only.

A November 1989 recording from the Gator Bowl, Jacksonville, Florida, on *Flashpoint*, found them doing it justice (not before time) with additional backing musicians and also a French horn player on stage at last. The 50 and Counting tour shows from October 2012 to July 2013, with English dates at the 0_2 Arena, Hyde Park and the Glastonbury Festival, had the additional benefits – at long last – of including the choral sections, courtesy of the Voce Chamber and London Youth Choirs. Jagger was also to be seen strumming an acoustic guitar as he sang the first verse and chorus, before taking it off to pace along the full length of the stage as usual while he continued with a hand mic. On a couple of dates on the American tour in December 2012, the band were joined for two shows by the Trinity Wall Street Choir, an eight-minute version, with one appearing on *Grrr Live!* By this time, it had long become part of Jagger's routine, during the extended fourth verse about the Chelsea Drugstore, to sing 'What's your favourite flavour?' and the audience would shout back, 'Cherry red!'

In addition to The Friends of Jo Cox collective's version mentioned above, over 80 others at last count, have tried their hand at it. Def Leppard took on the full 7½-minute version and released it as a bonus track on the deluxe edition of *Adrenalize* (1992), turning it into a wistful Celtic anthem with prominent mandolin and pennywhistle, courtesy of Irish band Hothouse Flowers. In 1970, P.P. Arnold recorded a four-minute take produced by Eric Clapton, featuring him and other members of Derek and the Dominos, with Bobby Keys on sax. It was part of an album featuring material produced mostly by Clapton or by Barry Gibb, recorded between 1969 and 1972, shelved for many years due to numerous record company shenanigans, and finally released in 2017 as *The Turning Tide*.

Live albums and movies: *Love You Live* (1977); *Flashpoint* (1991); *Rock and Roll Circus* (1968, released 1996); *Ladies And Gentlemen: The Rolling Stones; Havana Moon; Hyde Park Live; Brussels Affair; Grrr Live!*

Legacy

Let It Bleed is, in a way, a hard album to pigeonhole. It's not just rock but also semi-acoustic folk country, with a nod to Cajun at the same time. Is it also (or only) rock 'n' roll, or blues, with touches of psychedelia, jazz, and gospel here and there? Yes – it's the lot, all at once. As regards its pivotal place in popular music history and continuing legacy, that's a different matter. Put simply, the last great album of the 1960s, unleashed on an eager public and critical audience with just four weeks of the decade to go, it pointed the way to several musical directions of the 1970s. Moreover, with hindsight in the eyes of some critics and music historians, it was and would always remain one of the finest, if not *the* finest, made by the act who were just about to seize their place as the world's greatest rock 'n' roll band from their self-destructing rivals from Merseyside. When asked about it in July 1969, shortly before it was completed, an enthusiastic Richards told journalists that he thought it was 'the best stuff we have done so far. It's like a progression from *Beggars Banquet*, only heavier'.

Something, albeit briefly, has to be said about the way it inadvertently mirrored the times in which it was made. Those who are familiar with the long and complex history of The Rolling Stones will hardly need reminding that it was only just starting to fly out of the shops out of the shops as its creators were about to play the ill-fated Altamont show. In addition to the killing of Meredith Hunter, there were also two accidental deaths (a hit-and-run and a drug-fuelled drowning) at the scene. The Woodstock Festival in August 1969 had also been marred by fatalities, namely three deaths, two drug overdoses and one when a tractor accidentally ran over a sleeping attendee. The Stones were singing about violence, specifically rape and murder, and blood was spilled, although later adjudged an act of self-defence as opposed to murder. ('Gimme Shelter' was on the setlist, though the song they were playing at the time was 'Under my Thumb'). The Stones had looked over the abyss, and didn't like what they saw. Had it been provocative to perform a song with the line, 'it's just a shot away'? Jagger, who might have been Hunter's target, was reportedly nervous about live work for some time afterwards, and for a long time, they ensured that they remained behind barriers to prevent the wrong people from getting too close. The murder of John Lennon just over a decade later was a chilling reminder not to take chances.

The first week of December 1969 was certainly an important one in the group's long history. *Let It Bleed* was released in Britain on the 5th, and next day they played Altamont. The classic 'Brown Sugar' received its live premiere there, having been recorded at Muscle Shoals, Alabama, over 2-4 December, though it was not released until April 1971. An alternative version with Eric Clapton on slide guitar and Al Kooper on keyboards, taped at Richards' birthday party in December 1970, was finally made officially available in 2015.

Having disposed of the matter of life imitating art, what were the consequences of the album and its influences on what came afterwards? For 'the album', you could perhaps read 'the group's four albums, of which this was the second', but this was perhaps their artistic peak.

As for the musical legacy, the group had subtly shifted direction more than once during the seven years since they made their debut on stage in London. *Beggars Banquet* was the first album after their R'n'B-pop-psychedelia phase in which they retained elements of all three genres but at the same time carved out something more distinctive. *Let It Bleed* took it to a new level. The first and last tracks mirrored to perfection the unsettled era in which they were conceived and created, while the remaining seven spanned a remarkable range of genres.

Like The Beatles and Bob Dylan, The Rolling Stones were a huge influence on so many acts of the 1960s and 1970s. The album's nine richly-flavoured tracks touch so many genres, and, in doing so, showed that none of them need be mutually exclusive. Rock 'n' roll could go hand in hand with almost everything. Country rock was currently very much in vogue, encompassing everyone from The Band and The Byrds to Creedence Clearwater Revival and Grateful Dead, and The Rolling Stones' eighth album could undoubtedly take some of the credit. Gram Parsons, who had been briefly a Byrd and then a Flying Burrito Brother, became a friend of the group and spent some time with Richards in France while the group was recording *Exile on Main St* in 1971, although he was never a guest musician or singer on the album. On the other hand Eric Clapton played from time to time with the Stones in this era, to the extent of inviting speculation that he was being considered as a replacement for Brian Jones. His work around the time that he launched his solo career and fronted the short-lived Derek and the Dominos showed a pronounced love of country rock mingled with his lifelong blues inspiration, quite apart from the fact that he too would cover 'Love in Vain' one day.

If Britain's two top groups in 1969, alongside the Stones, were The Beatles (in the process of splitting) and new kids on the block, Led Zeppelin, at least some of their members had their finger on the pulse. Clapton was very much a common link with George Harrison, as a lifelong friend and one of the main guest musicians on *All Things Must Pass*, the triple album Harrison would release in 1970. It's easy to detect similarities between some songs on the record with tracks on *Let It Bleed*, such as 'Wah-Wah', also built around a guitar riff and with the same busy, bubbling, slightly funky rhythm as 'Monkey Man', the sweet pedal steel guitar-driven country ballad 'Behind That Locked Door' with 'You Got the Silver', and maybe even the massed multi-tracked vocal call-and-respond vocals on 'My Sweet Lord' with the choral sections on 'You Can't Always Get What You Want' – although Harrison specifically mentioned The Edwin Hawkins Singers' gospel anthem 'Oh Happy Day' as inspiration for the song.

Led Zeppelin's fourth album would have more acoustic numbers than usual, while years later, Plant would also give free rein to his love of country music on two albums that he recorded with Alison Krauss. As for the band, much as Richards might disparage them when talking to journalists, he always acknowledged his great respect for their guitarist and once said that 'Led Zeppelin is Jimmy Page'. When Richards walked in on one of their sessions in October 1974, it resulted in him, Page, Jagger, Ronnie Wood (still a member of The Faces at that time) and Ric Grech, former Family and Blind Faith bassist, creating the track 'Scarlet'. Apparently named after Page's daughter, it was described by its creators as having 'a cod-reggae feel', and would appear as a bonus track on the 2020 remastered reissue of *Goats Head Soup*.

It's safe to assume that some, if not all, of these acts were subconsciously influenced in some way by the album. Around the time of release, It was certainly a favourite on the turntable with Free, whose meteoric success in the summer of 1970 with 'All Right Now' and their third album *Fire And Water*, led to them being dubbed 'the new Rolling Stones' by the music press in a year when there were no new singles by Jagger, Richards & Co to compete. Rod Clements, bassist, fiddler and one of the main songwriters in Lindisfarne, was an avid Stones admirer who praised them 'from a rock and roll and lyrical point of view', and his songs 'The Road to Kingdom Come' and 'Don't Ask Me', on the Geordie folk-rock quintet's first three albums, both hinted at a strong influence. Not forgetting Rod Stewart, a highly-respected though then little-known singer renowned during his early career for a love of blues and folk, who had recently left The Jeff Beck Group and was about to record his first solo album – and who, once successful as a soloist as well as vocalist with The Faces, would often be compared with Mick Jagger. No wonder his guitarist, Ronnie Wood, would soon become a Rolling Stone.

While the Burritos and other contemporary country rock standard-bearers like Poco and Pure Prairie League all enjoyed moderate, if limited success, The Eagles would leave them all in the shade. From their formation in 1971, they were particularly keen to work with Glyn Johns and even uproot themselves for weeks at a time to go and record their first two albums at Olympic Studios in London, as it was the city where The Beatles and The Rolling Stones had recorded so many of their classics – and Johns was the man who had played such an important role as engineer with both acts.

The album has continued to cast its spell over those from younger generations, even punk musicians and their peers who might have professed to disown everything The Rolling Stones ever stood for. Mick Jones of The Clash admitted he adored the albums from their purple patch, while Jean-Jacques Burnel of The Stranglers said they were 'fantastic' in their early years. The Stones were sometimes guarded in their comments on the new wave, while Richards underlined the fact that the rebels from the class of '77 had something in common with himself and Jagger, even if they lacked their musical skills. Moreover, they were the only rock 'n' roll band ever arrested for urinating against a wall.

Younger groups from later years have been no less enthusiastic, and some of their music has shown a pronounced influence.

During the late 1980s, Ian Astbury and Jamie Stewart, vocalist and bassist respectively with The Cult, admitted that the sounds of the Stones, Cream, Zeppelin and Hendrix were all to be found on their latest album; they'd 'completely lost interest in British post-punk things'. In 1991, Primal Scream's *Screamadelica* instantly drew comparisons from critics, particularly in America, with late-1960s Stones. Guns 'n' Roses, who emerged at around the same time, almost seemed like a late 1980s reincarnation of them with their bad-boy behaviour as well as music that appealed to album-buying metalheads as well as singles lovers, while The Black Crowes could often be relied on to draw on the Jagger-Richards songbook, early 1970s era, for a cover version or two on stage. AC/DC were also fully paid-up fans, both winning the Richards and Watts seal of approval. On the Stones' Licks tour of 2003 Angus Young was invited to come and rehearse briefly and then on stage to jam with them on B.B. King's 'Rock Me Baby', and when Angus's elder brother Malcolm, the group's rhythm guitarist who had to retire from the band because of dementia, he found particular solace in being played Rolling Stones albums up during the last weeks before his death in 2017.

Members of two of America's newer indie rock bands have testified to their love for the album and the songs from it. From Nashville, Daniel Ellsworth, vocalist and keyboard player with Daniel Ellsworth & The Great Lakes, said that the first time he ever heard The Rolling Stones, it was 'You Can't Always Get What You Want' on a local radio station when he was about 14. He readily agreed that just like The Beatles, 'The Stones' influence on pop and rock music as we now know it is undeniable. They influence every rock band making music, whether we know it or not'. His favourite album of all time, by a long way, was *Let It Bleed*. 'After I heard 'You Can't Always Get What You Want', I had to have it. The whole album is magic'. Similar praise came from Julian Fader, drummer of Ava Luna, an indie band from Brooklyn, New York, who testified to the potency of one track in particular. 'My dad was always a Beatles guy, but I explicitly remember him playing me 'Monkey Man' at a very young age. I thought that piano intro was so sinister that it actually scared me'.

On *Beggars Banquet*, The Rolling Stones had delivered what would prove to be a solid, enduring classic. With *Let It Bleed*, an album written and recorded during a period of turmoil for the band with the departure and death of one member, they went one better, and the next three albums would prove it was no flash in the pan. The biggest rock 'n' roll band – apart from Led Zeppelin, there was no competition in the immediate post-Beatles era, at least until Queen arrived – would go on to celebrate fifty years in the business, even sixty, even if only two of the founder members were left by then. It might be hyperbole to suggest that it was this eighth album that made it all possible. Yet it was, without doubt, a towering musical achievement that cemented their place on the pedestal and remains as valid, powerful and as much a mirror of its times as it was the week it was released.

Sources

Books

Davis, S., *Old Gods Almost Dead: The 40-Year Odyssey Of The Rolling Stones* (Broadway, 2001)

Egan, S., *The Rolling Stones And The Making Of Let It Bleed* (Unanimous, 2005)

Richards, K. and Fox, J., *Life* (Weidenfeld & Nicolson, 2010)

Johns, G., *Sound Man* (Blue Rider, 2014)

Pilkington, S., *The Rolling Stones On Track: Every Album, Every Song* (Sonicbond, 2019)

Rolling Stones, The, *According To The Rolling Stones* (Chronicle, 2009)

Tobler, J., & Grundy, S., *The Record Producers* (BBC, 1982)

Wyman, B., *Rolling With The Stones* (Dorling Kindersley, 2002)

Magazines

Classic Rock
Disc And Music Echo
Melody Maker
New Musical Express
Record Collector
Rolling Stone
Sounds

Internet Sources

45cat
All Music Guide To Rock
Discogs
Guitar World
Rolling Stones Data
Secondhand Songs
Time Is On Our Side (The Rolling Stones Forever)
Ultimate Classic Rock

On Track Series

Allman Brothers Band – Andrew Wild 978-1-78952-252-5

Tori Amos – Lisa Torem 978-1-78952-142-9

Aphex Twin – Beau Waddell 978-1-78952-267-9

Asia – Peter Braidis 978-1-78952-099-6

Badfinger – Robert Day-Webb 978-1-878952-176-4

Barclay James Harvest – Keith And Monica Domone
978-1-78952-067-5

Beck – Arthur Lizie 978-1-78952-258-7

The Beatles – Andrew Wild 978-1-78952-009-5

The Beatles Solo 1969-1980 – Andrew Wild 978-1-78952-030-9

Blue Oyster Cult – Jacob Holm-Lupo 978-1-78952-007-1

Blur – Matt Bishop 978-178952-164-1

Marc Bolan And T.rex – Peter Gallagher 978-1-78952-124-5

Kate Bush – Bill Thomas 978-1-78952-097-2

Camel – Hamish Kuzminski 978-1-78952-040-8

Captain Beefheart – Opher Goodwin 978-1-78952-235-8

Caravan – Andy Boot 978-1-78952-127-6

Cardiacs – Eric Benac 978-1-78952-131-3

Nick Cave And The Bad Seeds – Dominic Sanderson
978-1-78952-240-2

Eric Clapton Solo – Andrew Wild 978-1-78952-141-2

The Clash – Nick Assirati 978-1-78952-077-4

Elvis Costello And The Attractions – Georg Purvis 978-1-78952-129-0

Crosby, Stills And Nash – Andrew Wild 978-1-78952-039-2

Creedence Clearwater Revival – Tony Thompson 978-178952-237-2

The Damned – Morgan Brown 978-1-78952-136-8

Deep Purple And Rainbow 1968-79 – Steve Pilkington
978-1-78952-002-6

Dire Straits – Andrew Wild 978-1-78952-044-6

The Doors – Tony Thompson 978-1-78952-137-5

Dream Theater – Jordan Blum 978-1-78952-050-7

Eagles – John Van Der Kiste 978-1-78952-260-0

Earth, Wind And Fire – Bud Wilkins 978-1-78952-272-3

Electric Light Orchestra – Barry Delve 978-1-78952-152-8

Emerson Lake And Palmer – Mike Goode 978-1-78952-000-2

Fairport Convention – Kevan Furbank 978-1-78952-051-4

Peter Gabriel – Graeme Scarfe 978-1-78952-138-2

Genesis – Stuart Macfarlane 978-1-78952-005-7

Gentle Giant – Gary Steel 978-1-78952-058-3

Gong – Kevan Furbank 978-1-78952-082-8
Green Day – William E. Spevack 978-1-78952-261-7
Hall And Oates – Ian Abrahams 978-1-78952-167-2
Hawkwind – Duncan Harris 978-1-78952-052-1
Peter Hammill – Richard Rees Jones 978-1-78952-163-4
Roy Harper – Opher Goodwin 978-1-78952-130-6
Jimi Hendrix – Emma Stott 978-1-78952-175-7
The Hollies – Andrew Darlington 978-1-78952-159-7
Horslips – Richard James 978-1-78952-263-1
The Human League And The Sheffield Scene –
Andrew Darlington 978-1-78952-186-3
The Incredible String Band – Tim Moon 978-1-78952-107-8
Iron Maiden – Steve Pilkington 978-1-78952-061-3
Joe Jackson – Richard James 978-1-78952-189-4
Jefferson Airplane – Richard Butterworth 978-1-78952-143-6
Jethro Tull – Jordan Blum 978-1-78952-016-3
Elton John In The 1970s – Peter Kearns 978-1-78952-034-7
Billy Joel – Lisa Torem 978-1-78952-183-2
Judas Priest – John Tucker 978-1-78952-018-7
Kansas – Kevin Cummings 978-1-78952-057-6
The Kinks – Martin Hutchinson 978-1-78952-172-6
Korn – Matt Karpe 978-1-78952-153-5
Led Zeppelin – Steve Pilkington 978-1-78952-151-1
Level 42 – Matt Philips 978-1-78952-102-3
Little Feat – Georg Purvis - 978-1-78952-168-9
Aimee Mann – Jez Rowden 978-1-78952-036-1
Joni Mitchell – Peter Kearns 978-1-78952-081-1
The Moody Blues – Geoffrey Feakes 978-1-78952-042-2
Motorhead – Duncan Harris 978-1-78952-173-3
Nektar – Scott Meze – 978-1-78952-257-0
New Order – Dennis Remmer – 978-1-78952-249-5
Nightwish – Simon Mcmurdo – 978-1-78952-270-9
Laura Nyro – Philip Ward 978-1-78952-182-5
Mike Oldfield – Ryan Yard 978-1-78952-060-6
Opeth – Jordan Blum 978-1-78-952-166-5
Pearl Jam – Ben L. Connor 978-1-78952-188-7
Tom Petty – Richard James 978-1-78952-128-3
Pink Floyd – Richard Butterworth 978-1-78952-242-6
The Police – Pete Braidis 978-1-78952-158-0
Porcupine Tree – Nick Holmes 978-1-78952-144-3

Queen – Andrew Wild 978-1-78952-003-3
Radiohead – William Allen 978-1-78952-149-8
Rancid – Paul Matts 989-1-78952-187-0
Renaissance – David Detmer 978-1-78952-062-0
Reo Speedwagon – Jim Romag 978-1-78952-262-4
The Rolling Stones 1963-80 – Steve Pilkington 978-1-78952-017-0
The Smiths And Morrissey – Tommy Gunnarsson
978-1-78952-140-5
Spirit – Rev. Keith A. Gordon – 978-1-78952- 248-8
Stackridge – Alan Draper 978-1-78952-232-7
Status Quo The Frantic Four Years – Richard James
978-1-78952-160-3
Steely Dan – Jez Rowden 978-1-78952-043-9
Steve Hackett – Geoffrey Feakes 978-1-78952-098-9
Tears For Fears – Paul Clark - 978-178952-238-9
Thin Lizzy – Graeme Stroud 978-1-78952-064-4
Tool – Matt Karpe 978-1-78952-234-1
Toto – Jacob Holm-Lupo 978-1-78952-019-4
U2 – Eoghan Lyng 978-1-78952-078-1
Ufo – Richard James 978-1-78952-073-6
Van Der Graaf Generator – Dan Coffey 978-1-78952-031-6
Van Halen – Morgan Brown – 9781-78952-256-3
The Who – Geoffrey Feakes 978-1-78952-076-7
Roy Wood And The Move – James R Turner 978-1-78952-008-8
Yes – Stephen Lambe 978-1-78952-001-9
Frank Zappa 1966 To 1979 – Eric Benac 978-1-78952-033-0
Warren Zevon – Peter Gallagher 978-1-78952-170-2
10cc – Peter Kearns 978-1-78952-054-5

Decades Series
The Bee Gees In The 1960s – Andrew Mon Hughes Et Al
978-1-78952-148-1
The Bee Gees In The 1970s – Andrew Mon Hughes Et Al
978-1-78952-179-5
Black Sabbath In The 1970s – Chris Sutton 978-1-78952-171-9
Britpop – Peter Richard Adams And Matt Pooler 978-1-78952-169-6
Phil Collins In The 1980s – Andrew Wild 978-1-78952-185-6
Alice Cooper In The 1970s – Chris Sutton 978-1-78952-104-7
Alice Cooper In The 1980s – Chris Sutton 978-1-78952-259-4
Curved Air In The 1970s – Laura Shenton 978-1-78952-069-9

Donovan In The 1960s – Jeff Fitzgerald 978-1-78952-233-4
Bob Dylan In The 1980s – Don Klees 978-1-78952-157-3
Brian Eno In The 1970s – Gary Parsons 978-1-78952-239-6
Faith No More In The 1990s – Matt Karpe 978-1-78952-250-1
Fleetwood Mac In The 1970s – Andrew Wild 978-1-78952-105-4
Fleetwood Mac In The 1980s – Don Klees 978-178952-254-9
Focus In The 1970s – Stephen Lambe 978-1-78952-079-8
Free And Bad Company In The 1970s – John Van Der Kiste
978-1-78952-178-8
Genesis In The 1970s – Bill Thomas 978178952-146-7
George Harrison In The 1970s – Eoghan Lyng 978-1-78952-174-0
Kiss In The 1970s – Peter Gallagher 978-1-78952-246-4
Manfred Mann's Earth Band In The 1970s – John Van Der Kiste
978178952-243-3
Marillion In The 1980s – Nathaniel Webb 978-1-78952-065-1
Van Morrison In The 1970s – Peter Childs - 978-1-78952-241-9
Mott The Hoople And Ian Hunter In The 1970s –
John Van Der Kiste 978-1-78-952-162-7
Pink Floyd In The 1970s – Georg Purvis 978-1-78952-072-9
Suzi Quatro In The 1970s – Darren Johnson 978-1-78952-236-5
Queen In The 1970s – James Griffiths 978-1-78952-265-5
Roxy Music In The 1970s – Dave Thompson 978-1-78952-180-1
Slade In The 1970s – Darren Johnson 978-1-78952-268-6
Status Quo In The 1980s – Greg Harper 978-1-78952-244-0
Tangerine Dream In The 1970s – Stephen Palmer
978-1-78952-161-0
The Sweet In The 1970s – Darren Johnson 978-1-78952-139-9
Uriah Heep In The 1970s – Steve Pilkington 978-1-78952-103-0
Van Der Graaf Generator In The 1970s – Steve Pilkington
978-1-78952-245-7
Rick Wakeman In The 1970s – Geoffrey Feakes 978-1-78952-264-8
Yes In The 1980s – Stephen Lambe With David Watkinson
978-1-78952-125-2

On Screen Series
Carry On... – Stephen Lambe 978-1-78952-004-0
David Cronenberg – Patrick Chapman 978-1-78952-071-2
Doctor Who: The David Tennant Years – Jamie Hailstone
978-1-78952-066-8
James Bond – Andrew Wild 978-1-78952-010-1

Monty Python – Steve Pilkington 978-1-78952-047-7
Seinfeld Seasons 1 To 5 – Stephen Lambe 978-1-78952-012-5

Other Books

1967: A Year In Psychedelic Rock – Kevan Furbank
978-1-78952-155-9
1970: A Year In Rock – John Van Der Kiste 978-1-78952-147-4
1973: The Golden Year Of Progressive Rock – Geoffrey Feakes
978-1-78952-165-8
Babysitting A Band On The Rocks – G.D. Praetorius
978-1-78952-106-1
Eric Clapton Sessions – Andrew Wild 978-1-78952-177-1
Derek Taylor: For Your Radioactive Children –
Andrew Darlington 978-1-78952-038-5
The Golden Road: The Recording History Of The Grateful Dead –
John Kilbride 978-1-78952-156-6
Iggy And The Stooges On Stage 1967-1974 – Per Nilsen
978-1-78952-101-6
Jon Anderson And The Warriors – The Road To Yes –
David Watkinson 978-1-78952-059-0
Magic: The David Paton Story – David Paton 978-1-78952-266-2
Misty: The Music Of Johnny Mathis – Jakob Baekgaard
978-1-78952-247-1
Nu Metal: A Definitive Guide – Matt Karpe 978-1-78952-063-7
Tommy Bolin: In And Out Of Deep Purple – Laura Shenton
978-1-78952-070-5
Maximum Darkness – Deke Leonard 978-1-78952-048-4
The Twang Dynasty – Deke Leonard 978-1-78952-049-1

and many more to come!

Would you like to write for Sonicbond Publishing?

We are mainly a music publisher, but we also occasionally publish in other genres including film and television. At Sonicbond Publishing we are always on the look-out for authors, particularly for our two main series, On Track and Decades.

Mixing fact with in depth analysis, the On Track series examines the entire recorded work of a particular musical artist or group. All genres are considered from easy listening and jazz to 60s soul to 90s pop, via rock and metal.

The Decades series singles out a particular decade in an artist or group's history and focuses on that decade in more detail than may be allowed in the On Track series.

While professional writing experience would, of course, be an advantage, the most important qualification is to have real enthusiasm and knowledge of your subject. First-time authors are welcomed, but the ability to write well in English is essential.

Sonicbond Publishing has distribution throughout Europe and North America, and all our books are also published in E-book form. Authors will be paid a royalty based on sales of their book.

Further details about our books are available from www.sonicbondpublishing.com. To contact us, complete the contact form there or email info@sonicbondpublishing.co.uk